The ministry of Child Evangelism [Fellowship has been part of] my life for as long as I can remember. [Growing] up in Argentina, my mom organize[d Good News Clubs in our] neighborhood. Children filled our home and heard the Gospel for the first time. I remember CEF missionaries visiting our small town. Years later CEF sponsored a concert tour for me throughout Argentina, enabling me to see firsthand their passion for reaching children.

Today CEF is needed more than ever. In a world where children are too often seen as a nuisance and a burden, CEF reflects the heart of our Lord Jesus. They welcome the little ones and offer them the glorious hope found in the Gospel of Jesus Christ.

—Steve Green
CHRISTIAN ARTIST AND SONGWRITER

When it comes to creatively and compassionately telling the Gospel story to boys and girls, no one does it better than Child Evangelism Fellowship. The CEF team has a wealth of ideas and resources which will help any church skillfully present the Good News of Jesus to today's children!

—Joni Eareckson Tada
FOUNDER/CEO OF JONI AND FRIENDS INTERNATIONAL DISABILITY CENTER

I came to know Christ as my Savior at age five because a children's evangelist cared enough about kids to come to my church and preach the Gospel. I was reached when I had my whole life ahead of me to serve the Lord. That's why I endorse the outstanding work of Child Evangelism Fellowship.

—Dr. Woodrow Kroll
FORMER PRESIDENT AND SENIOR BIBLE TEACHER
AT BACK TO THE BIBLE INTERNATIONAL

I have had the privilege to know intimately each of the past presidents of Child Evangelism Fellowship. During my freshmen year in college, I became acquainted with the founder of CEF, J. Irvin Overholtzer. Over the years I've worked alongside five CEF presidents—men of faith and compassion. Each of them was deeply concerned for the lostness of children.

A new day dawned on CEF when God laid His hand on Reese Kauffman, appointing him the ninth and longest serving president. Reese has brought vision, fervency and a spiritual entrepreneurial zeal rarely found in Christian ministries. I applaud Reese and his wife Linda for their dedication and commitment to CEF.

I thank the Lord for the 26 years Reese has not only kept his hand on the helm but also has undauntedly guided it prayerfully along paths heretofore never trodden. As has been said, "Beaten paths are for beaten men." Reese has been a trailblazer, taking us into spheres of ministry that have touched the lives of millions of souls around the world. I join with others in dedicating this book to a man whose heart is focused on the souls of children.

—Dr. Carl H. Smith
ROMANIAN TRAINING MINISTRIES, INC.

I am personally thankful to God for the ministry of CEF! Their passion to share the Gospel with children is unmatched by any organization in the world. I've witnessed the fruit of their ministry in churches, the Indianapolis community, public schools and the mission field. Millions of children will be in Heaven because of God's work through CEF.

—Mark Vroegop
LEAD PASTOR, COLLEGE PARK CHURCH, INDIANAPOLIS, IN

EVERY
CHILD
EVERY
NATION
EVERY
DAY

The Story of Child Evangelism
Fellowship and Its President,
Reese Kauffman

Robert J. Morgan

The following are registered trademarks of Child Evangelism Fellowship Inc. and are used throughout this book:

Child Evangelism Fellowship® CEF® Good News Club® 5-Day Club® Wonderzone® Camp Good News® Children's Ministries Institute® CMI® Christian Youth in Action® Truth Chasers Club® Good News Across America®

The following are trademarks of Child Evangelism Fellowship Inc. and are used throughout this book:

Teaching Children Effectively™ TCE™ GNC™

CEF Press® is a publishing ministry of Child Evangelism Fellowship Inc. CEF Press develops, produces and distributes a variety of publications for the purpose of helping evangelize children. To order materials or receive a free catalog, go to cefpress.com or call 1-800-748-7710.

First Edition 2015

Designed by Brent Hautle

Edited by Rick Bunch and Deborah Koenig

ISBN: 978-1-55976-392-9

Contents

Part 3: Jesus Christ and the Miracle of Child Evangelism Fellowship

Part 4: Biblical Convictions and the Ministry of Child Evangelism Fellowship

Majoring on Minors

THE THIN MAN AWOKE TO FIND HIS ROOM AS COLD AS AN ICEBOX. A snowstorm was battering his town of Colchester, sixty miles from London, and it was almost as frigid inside the house as it was outside. It took determined effort to roll out of bed on that blizzard-blanketed Sunday morning January 6, 1850.

This simple fellow—no one remembers his name or vocation, though it's thought he was a cobbler or a tailor, or perhaps he earned his living growing cabbages—shoved himself into his clothes, pressed his feet into his boots, wrapped his warmest coat around him, and stepped out of his cottage. Colchester was a whitened ghost town. Arriving at the Artillery Street Primitive Methodist Church, he knew it would be a lean Sunday. Not even the pastor showed up—only a dozen or so stalwart souls who huddled near the front of the chapel and eventually settled into the worship service as best they could.

Meanwhile, a local boy was also fighting the blizzard, heading to another church some distance away. Charlie, age 15, on midwinter break from boarding school, was terribly unhappy and battling depression. His problems were spiritual in nature, as he well knew; he craved a sense of God's mercy and love. But hopelessness hung over his heart, and his spirits were as frozen as his breath in the air. The storm got the best of him that day, and the boy ducked into an alley to escape the biting wind. Seeing the sign for Artillery Street Primitive Methodist Church, he pushed through the door and took a seat in the back beneath the balcony.

At length, the thin man stepped to the pulpit and attempted to give an impromptu sermon. Finding a text in his Bible, he read Isaiah 45:22: "Look unto me, and be ye saved, all the ends of the earth."[1] He seemed ill-prepared to preach as he stammered and stuttered, trying to spin out a brief message.

As Charlie recalled, "He did not even pronounce the words rightly, but that did not matter. There was, I thought, a glimpse of hope for me in that text. The preacher began thus: 'My dear friends, this is a very simple text indeed. It says, "Look...." Well, a man needn't go to college to learn to look. You may be the biggest fool, and yet you can look.... Anyone can look; even a child can look. But then the text says, "Look unto Me." Ay! Many of ye are lookin' to yourselves but it's no use lookin' there. You'll never find any comfort in yourselves.... Christ says, "Look to Me.... I am sweatin' great drops of blood. Look unto Me; I am hangin' on the cross. Look unto Me; I am dead and buried. Look unto Me; I rise again. Look unto Me; I ascend to Heaven. Look unto Me; I am sittin' at the Father's right hand. O poor sinner, look unto Me! Look unto Me!"'"

The man extemporized along those lines for about ten minutes, then seemed to run out of steam until he spied the boy beneath the gallery. With a surge of inspiration, he said, "Young man, you look very miserable."

Though surprised to be singled out, Charlie realized the words were true.

"Young man, you look very miserable, and you always will be miserable—miserable in life and miserable in death—if you don't obey my text; but if you obey now, this moment, you will be saved." Then, lifting up his hands he shouted, "Young man, look to Jesus Christ. Look! Look! Look! You have nothin' to do but to look and live."

The words struck like lightning. The boy later said, "Oh, I looked... Then and there the cloud was gone, the darkness had rolled away, and at that moment I saw the sun...and I could have risen that instant and sung with the most enthusiastic of them of the precious blood of Christ and the simple faith that looks alone to Him."[2]

That was the moment the 15-year-old was saved, and it was one of the greatest days in the history of English Christianity. Young Charles Haddon Spurgeon left that chapel aflame for Christ. Soon he was preaching his own sermons and telling others to look to Jesus. Even as a teenager, his oratorical powers were mesmerizing. Before long, no building in England could hold the crowds wanting to hear him.

At the age of 19, Spurgeon became pastor of London's famous New Park Street Chapel, the largest Baptist congregation in London. Within a few years he was preaching to 6,000 people every Sunday, and this was well before the days of microphones or megachurches.

Spurgeon's printed ministry took his words even further. Every week his sermons were transcribed, published, translated into various languages, and sent around the world. This has made him the most widely read preacher in the history of Christianity.[3]

Spurgeon died in 1892 at the age of 57. He had worn himself out. But several decades later, a copy of one of his books ended up on the desk of a frustrated, aging California pastor named Jesse Irvin Overholtzer. Though Overholtzer had worked hard and tried his best, he felt he had little to show for his ministry. Unlike Spurgeon, his labor had yielded scant fruitfulness. Looking for encouragement, Overholtzer was working his way through Spurgeon's printed sermons, underlining key phrases and uplifting insights.

One day, as Jesse pored over Spurgeon's sermons he was jolted by 16 words that shocked him as though they held an electric charge. In the midst of one of his sermons, Spurgeon had made this declaration:

A child of five, if properly instructed,
can as readily believe and be regenerated as anyone.

That was news to Overholtzer. His austere denominational background had offered him no training in children's work. Preaching and evangelism, he thought, should be aimed at adults. At first, Overholtzer felt stung by Spurgeon's assertion. He wanted to argue with it. He told himself Spurgeon was wrong, that a child of five could not possibly have a life-changing, lifelong spiritual encounter with Christ. But the words kept pricking him, and he finally decided to put them to the test.

Overholtzer's first prospect was a nine-year-old boy. As simply and carefully as possible, he explained the Gospel—and to his amazement the boy readily put his faith in Jesus Christ. Soon a ten-year-old girl named Ruby did the same. In short order, 21 children had professed Christ as their Savior, and some began leading their parents to Christ. Overholtzer was set afire for child evangelism. His plan of ministry began to define itself, and in May of 1937 he founded an organization for the sole purpose of evangelizing and discipling youngsters—Child Evangelism Fellowship.

Overholtzer traveled across the United States promoting his work. Soon his vision swept beyond the borders of America. Unable to enter Europe or Asia because of World War II, he set his sights on South America. As the movement spread to Argentina, two women—Theda Krieger and Margaret Tyson—took up the work of evangelizing children in Buenos Aires. One day they met several children of the Palau family. Luis Palau, a teenager at the time, was eager to learn how to lead others to Christ. Theda and Margaret taught him how to share the Gospel, saying, "If you can lead a 12-year-old boy to Christ, you can lead the Queen of England to the Savior."

Young Luis studied the verses that would help him clearly and simply share the Gospel. He learned them well. Tutored by these two CEF missionaries, he started leading others to Christ, beginning with five boys in his neighborhood. Thus commenced a vast ministry that has spanned the globe for over 60 years. Luis Palau, one of the world's foremost evangelists, has shared the Gospel in person with more than a billion people at evangelistic events in 72 countries. Over a million people have reportedly received Christ under Luis's ministry! What an unlikely chain of events! Over the course of 150 years, a cause-and-effect series of blessings snapped into place, one after the other, to change the world. From an unschooled layman in Colchester...to a far-famed preacher in London...to a defeated pastor in California...to a pair of single missionaries in Argentina...to a worldwide evangelist reaching a billion people around the world.

> **From an unschooled layman in Colchester...to a far-famed preacher in London...to a defeated pastor in California...to a pair of single missionaries in Argentina... to a worldwide evangelist reaching a billion people around the world.**

And right in the middle of it all: Child Evangelism Fellowship, the world's foremost mission to children. As CEF has learned through decades of experience, one never knows the domino effect that begins when one wins a girl and boy to Christ, whether the child is 5 or 15. If there ever was an organization that majored on minors, it's Child Evangelism Fellowship.

How vital for every Christian to join the cause of proclaiming Christ to the newest and youngest among us! Each of us can be a link in a chain of evangelism, whatever our talents, background, education, failure or fame. That's why we roll out of bed on cold mornings. That's why we tell people to look to Jesus even if we stutter and stammer while doing so. That's why we don't grow weary in the Lord's work, for we know we'll reap a harvest if we don't give up. But our prospects are brightest when we understand this wonderful truth: even a child can look. A child of 5, if properly instructed, can as readily believe and be regenerated as anyone.

This is a ministry you must know, a cause you should embrace, a job you can do. Children are the most productive yet the most forgotten mission field in the world. Child evangelism is the greatest work on Earth. There have never been so many youngsters—over 2.6 billion of them.[4] They have never been so needy and the need has never been so urgent. The longer people live, the more difficult it is to reach them with the Gospel, which is their only hope for life and joy. How critical to establish a spiritual foundation for life while young! How vital to remember our Creator in the days of our youth, as Ecclesiastes 12:1 commands.

Someone said, "Children do not make up 100 percent of the population, but they do make up 100 percent of the future."[5] One never knows the chain reaction that occurs when a young person is won to the Lord. We never know what we've wrought for the Kingdom when a child comes to Christ. The echo effect grows with time, and the results multiply from now to eternity. Only Heaven can calculate the totality of our labor in children's work and our efforts in child evangelism. Don't underestimate how God can win and use a single child. Don't undervalue the joy of sowing the Gospel into a child's heart. Don't minimize how He can use you to advance the Gospel to little ones.

This is the mission of Child Evangelism Fellowship, taking the Good News of Jesus Christ to... Every Child, Every Nation, Every Day.

The Trouble with Children

THE TROUBLE WITH CHILDREN IS THAT CHILDREN ARE IN TROUBLE IN TODAY'S WORLD. Horrendous threats are encircling them like vultures, and their bodies, minds, and souls are at risk. Although they're the most innocent souls on the planet, they're the most endangered people on Earth.

During the last 50 years, our world has been in a moral and spiritual death spiral, with children as helpless victims. In the Western culture, school children are exposed to things never imagined by earlier generations. A pipeline of secular sewage is pouring filth into their tender minds—pornography, violence, secularism, agnosticism, atheism, godless entertainment, non-stop advertising, and every form of immorality conceived by human imagination.[6]

> **During the last 50 years, our world has been in a moral and spiritual death spiral, with children as helpless victims.**

With the collapse of the Judeo-Christian foundation of morality, which has undergirded western civilization for millennia, a fanatical brand of secularism has flooded the vacuum—filling textbooks, entertainment venues, social media, and popular culture with one dominate thought—there is no God, no hope, no eternity, and no basis for moral absolutes. We are not made in God's image, we're told; we are accidental products of random mutations that emerged from primordial sludge, destined to exist and die in a perishing universe that has no ultimate purpose. Our morality, then, can be whatever we wish. Since there is no God, there is no godliness. We can live autonomously and however we want to, since nothing matters in the long run.

Spiritual foundations are no longer established in youngsters' hearts, forcing children to build lives without the underpinnings of Scripture. Our schools are filled with profanity and sexuality, yet in those same classrooms the Bible is banned and prayer is forbidden. Imagine a nation in which the words "Oh my God" are widely spoken as an exclamatory oath in school hallways and platforms and lecterns, but those same words are illegal and forbidden when uttered as a prayer.

A large number of students in America's schools are threatened or injured each year with weapons such as guns, knives, or clubs on school property. Many students miss schooldays because they feel unsafe at school or on the way there.[7] We never know when another horrendous school shooting will capture the headlines.[8] Bullying is rampant, peer victimization is a constant threat, and gangs and gang violence grip many schoolyards and neighborhoods.

Inside the walls of many homes, family life is unhappy or nonexistent, and we're facing an onslaught of child abuse in all its worst forms. One in seven Americans will experience some form of maltreatment as children.[9] In America, more than three million cases of child abuse and neglect are reported annually, involving an estimated six million children.[10] A known case of child abuse occurs every ten seconds, and more than five children die every day from abuse.[11]

> **Inside the walls of many homes, family life is unhappy or nonexistent, and we're facing an onslaught of child abuse in all its worst forms.**

In many international locations the news is far worse. According to sources in the media, over 80 percent of the Palestinian children in Gaza have witnessed acts of violence and have seen friends or family members killed, blown up, or burned alive. Never mind the politics of it—children throughout the Middle East and in many regions of the world have suffered sustained post-traumatic stress due to wars and rumors of war.[12] Reports from the Middle East give blood-curdling details of children being subjected to torture and sexual violence as civil wars grind on in various failed nations. Just about every armed group in Syria has been listed by the United Nations as "known perpetrators of grave violations against children." According to the UN, Syrian children have been beaten with metal cables and whips. Electrical shocks have been applied to their bodies, including their genitals. Some have had their fingernails and toenails ripped out.[13] In areas overrun by jihadists, there have been reports of children being beheaded, crucified, and buried alive. This is painful to write but impossible to ignore.

The assault against the world's most innocent people—our youngsters—is the purest global evil of our time. For a moment let's forget about the politics of international immigration. In your mind's eye, picture the face of a single child—an anonymous face, dirty, dazed—being shuffled by illegal traffickers from Central America to the United States, or from Central Asia to the United Kingdom. Why is it the children who become pawns in a world of sordid political confusion and military misdeeds? Of the estimated 44 million refugees in the world, 80 percent are women and children.[14]

Worldwide, the trafficking of human beings has surpassed the drug trade to become the second largest source of money for organized crime (just behind illegal arms trading).[15] Fifty percent of these victims are children.[16] Approximately 30 million youngsters have lost their childhood to sexual exploitation over the past three decades.[17] According to UNICEF, there are an estimated two million young victims of sexual exploitation every year, though the numbers are undoubtedly much higher. In Indonesia, 30 percent of all prostitutes are younger than 18, and some are as young as 10. Sexual tourism is one of the fastest growing segments of the travel industry, especially in locations like Bali and Lombok.[18]

There are an estimated 151 million orphans in the world.[19] Many of them are trapped in loveless hovels and caught in a cycle of institutionalization, poverty, HIV/AIDS, and slavery. Who can begin to describe the horrors of what happens to children coerced by wicked warlords to be child soldiers? It's evil beyond evil.

Additionally, according to UNICEF, 22,000 children die each day due to poverty, and they "die quietly in some of the poorest villages on Earth, far removed from the scrutiny and the conscience of the world. Being meek and weak in life makes these dying multitudes even more invisible in death."[20] Malnutrition is an underlying cause of death for 2.6 million children each year,[21] and one in four of the world's children are stunted in body and brain growth due to hunger.[22]

Many agencies have mobilized to help children at every level. We should praise God for everyone providing humanitarian, philanthropic, legal, nutritional, medical, and educational assistance to children anywhere in the world. These are today's heroes—those who feed, clothe, educate, rescue, and care for the least among us. But behind all these dire needs is a spiritual hunger that can only be filled with the hope of Jesus Christ. There's a need for the Good News. Our most basic need is for a spiritual foundation based on the love of God.

Sharing the Gospel of Jesus with children is the distinctive mission of Child Evangelism Fellowship. This is our calling. We want every child to experience the reality of the little song that says, "Jesus loves me, this I know / For the Bible tells me so."[23] You would think that anyone seeking to help the children of the world would be applauded, lauded, encouraged, and supported, wouldn't you? Can you imagine a more comforting message than:

Jesus loves the little children, all the children of the world.
Red and yellow, black and white, they are precious in His sight.[24]

Yet CEF has faced increased pushback in recent years for nothing more than sharing the Good News of Christ with youngsters for whom He died. Recently CEF took the message of the Gospel to a major American city and encountered an interesting range of reactions. Many people were welcoming, but a handful of opponents were vocal, adversarial, and inclined to use phrases like "religious extremists" and "hardcore fundamentalist indoctrination," charging that CEF "terrorizes children" with "toxic fear-based doctrines" that can cause "trauma in children that can last into adulthood." Legal threats were thrown about like hot potatoes.

Undeterred, CEF missionaries went about their mission without reacting, issuing only a simple statement: "Child Evangelism Fellowship is a historic ministry that believes God loves both children and adults, and He wants to give them a spiritual and moral foundation for life. Children are mentioned about 100 times in the Gospels, and Jesus said, 'Let the little children come unto me.' For nearly 2,000 years, Christians have been spreading the Good News of Jesus Christ to adults and children alike, and for decades Child Evangelism Fellowship has been telling children around the world about the love of Jesus. We do not pressure or coerce children, and we respect the wishes of their parents or guardians. We have a wonderful message from Scripture, and we are happy to share it with those wanting to hear. Since children establish moral values early in life, they have a right to hear the Gospel if they desire, and we have a biblical obligation and the constitutional right to share the message of Jesus. We have 80 years of testimonies from people whose lives have been positively impacted by our message. Our goal, when our mission here is over, is to leave this city a happier place with healthier children and stronger homes. We appreciate the opportunity to serve here.'"

That may not satisfy the critics, but the Apostle Paul and Peter ran into the same antagonism in the first century and it didn't stop them, either. Our God-given mission is to reach every child, every nation, every day with the Good News of Jesus Christ, for behind our world's vast physical, educational, and moral need is an enormous spiritual vacuum. The problem resides in the human heart—and no statesman however gifted, no diplomat however eloquent, no educator however lauded—can change the heart. Only our Lord Jesus Christ can do that. He said in Matthew 15:19: "For out of the heart come evil thoughts, murder, adultery, sexual immorality, theft, false witness, slander."

All of our problems are, at their roots, spiritual. The one thing the children on Earth need more than anything else is Jesus and His mercy, Jesus and His love. They need the grace of a loving Savior and the Heaven He came to provide. They need the bread from above and the water of life and the hope of the One who called Himself the "Light of the World." They need people to love them in Jesus' name.

Children have Jesus-shaped hearts, and by the very nature of childhood they are open and eager for the kind of divine love offered by the Lord Jesus. That's why Christ said, "You must let little children come to me, and you must never stop them. The kingdom of Heaven belongs to little children like these" (Matthew 19:14).[25]

Informal studies conducted by Child Evangelism Fellowship missionaries through the years showed that one percent of Christians say they trusted Christ as Savior by age four; 10 percent between the ages of 15 and 30; and 4 percent were saved after age 30. But a whopping 85 percent trusted Christ while they were between the ages of 4 and 14.[26]

Several years ago, missionary strategist Luis Bush coined the phrase "The 10/40 Window" to describe the part of the globe containing the largest population of unreached and non-Christian people in the world. This designation refers to those living in the eastern hemisphere between 10 and 40 degrees north of the equator, a geographical rectangle that includes most of North Africa, the Middle East, and southern Asia.

Recently Bush has focused his attention on a new zone of opportunity—"The 4/14 Window." He introduced the term at a conference in Colorado Springs, inspired by the informal observations by CEF missionaries and others that approximately 85 percent of those coming to Christ do so between the ages of 4 and 14.[27] Bush urges people to consider the strategic importance and potential of the millions of children in "The 4/14 Window," saying, "It is crucial that missions efforts be reprioritized and redirected toward the 4/14 age group worldwide."[28]

Child Evangelism Fellowship is one ministry that doesn't need to reprioritize or redirect its efforts. It's been targeting the 4/14 window for the better part of a century. This book is a call to all of us to redouble our efforts and rededicate ourselves daily to this cause. When we evangelize girls and boys, we're reaching the most receptive audience in the world. No demographic on Earth is as open to the Gospel as those between the approximate ages of 5 to 15. Yet most children in America seldom or never attend church, and most children in the world grow up without hearing the wondrous message of the old rugged cross.

This is the decade of decision in a person's life. When we emerge from childhood, our morals are largely set, our spiritual direction is mostly determined, and our choices are largely made. When we reach out to children, we're impacting those with much of their life still before them. That's why the Psalmist prayed so earnestly, "Even when I am old and gray, do not forsake me, my God, till I declare Your power to the next generation, Your mighty acts to all who are to come" (Psalm 71:18).[29]

Moses prayed, "Satisfy us in our earliest youth with your loving-kindness, giving us constant joy to the end of our lives... let our children see glorious things... let the Lord our God favor us and give us success" (Psalm 90:14-17).[30]

Jesus said, "See that you do not despise one of these little ones. For I tell you that in heaven their angels always see the face of my Father who is in heaven... So it is not the will of my Father who is in heaven that one of these little ones should perish" (Matthew 18:10, 14).

"If you want to shape a person's life," wrote researcher George Barna, "whether you are most concerned about his or her moral, spiritual, intellectual, emotional or economic development—it is during these crucial eight years [from ages 5 to 12] that lifelong habits, values, beliefs, and attitudes are formed."[31]

If children have a clear and proper exposure to the Good News of Jesus, they are remarkably receptive. There's no time to waste, for a person's conscious spiritual and moral development starts as early as age two—maybe even earlier, much earlier. The moral foundations are generally determined before age ten. "By age nine," says Barna, "most children have their spiritual moorings in place." By 13, a person's spiritual identity is largely established.[32]

"If you want to have a lasting influence upon the world," wrote Barna, "you must invest in people's lives; and if you want to maximize that investment, then you must invest in those people while they are young.... Children matter to God because He loves them and wants them to experience the best, right from the start of their lives."[33]

Since children are more open to the Gospel than any other demographic group in the world, and since the childhood years pass quickly, we're ministering through a window that is quickly closing. Time is short. The vast majority of Christians claim to have been converted in childhood with decisions that have lasted a lifetime, yet the greatest effort of most churches and evangelistic organizations is aimed at adults—a vital but far less responsive audience.

> **Since children are more open to the Gospel than any other demographic group in the world... we're ministering through a window that is quickly closing.**

Child Evangelism Fellowship is the world's largest mission to children and one of its oldest, with missionaries in 192 countries, and soon, God willing, in every nation around the globe. In 2014, over 300,000 missionaries were trained and CEF staff and volunteers presented the Gospel to 19.9 million children in person—with over six million recorded professions of faith. We're driven by a sense of urgency. We've got to reach the children while we still can. Our dream is to personally share the Gospel of

Jesus Christ with 100 million children every year, using proven CEF missionaries and materials.

Last year, at an informational dinner for Child Evangelism Fellowship, one of the guests took in the story of CEF, smiled with insight and enthusiasm, and exclaimed, "This is the greatest ministry in the world!" At first, those sitting near him thought he was simply caught up in the moment. But I confess I'm caught up in the moment too. I feel as he does. After all, what other organization in the world is historic in its mission, global in its outreach, targeting the most receptive but neglected mission field on Earth, sharing the Gospel with tens of millions, and recording hundreds of thousands of conversions to Christ every year—year after year—among a demographic having a lifetime of service ahead of them?

This book will share the story of Child Evangelism Fellowship, its heritage, its people and passion, and its vision for the future in seeking to reach Every Child, Every Nation, Every Day. The youngsters of Earth deserve to know that Jesus loves them.

And we love them, too.

PART 1

Jesse Overholtzer and the Message of Child Evangelism Fellowship

CHAPTER 1
The Moldable Years

THE LIFE OF JESSE OVERHOLTZER (1877-1955) IS A LESSON IN LONGEVITY AND LEGACY, PROVING THAT OUR LATTER YEARS CAN BE THE MOST PRODUCTIVE OF ALL, A SEASON IN WHICH ALL OUR EXPERIENCES ACCRUE TO MAKE US MORE USABLE THAN EVER. Overholtzer was 60 years old when he launched Child Evangelism Fellowship, and he directed its ministries until he was 75. He never attended a Bible school or seminary, his voice was described as weak, and frustration marked much of his ministry. Yet his drive to bring boys and girls to Christ changed the world.

Overholtzer's father, Samuel Overholtzer, was born in Pennsylvania's Lancaster County but moved to northwest Illinois as a young man. When Samuel was 21, he married his 17-year-old sweetheart, Maria. They attended a Brethren Church. The Brethren were pacifists, which led to a crisis during the Civil War. The Overholtzers didn't believe in taking human life, even in armed conflict. When the Union began drafting young men to fight in the Civil War, Sam, 24, saw only one option—to take his pregnant wife and three children and to move as far away from Ilinois as possible.

Almost overnight, Sam and Maria bundled up their children, sold their farm, abandoned their home, bought a prairie schooner, and joined a wagon train. They pulled out of town on an April morning in 1864. The caravan pushed westward, forded the Mississippi River, and plowed into the West, wanting to cross the Sierra Nevada Mountains before winter. Because the wagons were too big for the mountain passes, they had to be dismantled and lowered in pieces over cliffs and precipices; but the group made it to California before the harsh snows blocked their path.

Finally—after a six-month journey without a single loss of life—they crested the last hill and saw the spreading Sacramento Valley. Sam claimed a government homestead along the Sacramento River and tried to build a farm. When the area proved to be a flood plain, he moved his family to the nearby San Joaquin Valley. There, near the town of Banta, Jesse Irvin Overholtzer was born on July 20, 1877. The family subsequently moved to a farm outside the city of Covina, where Jesse grew up as the seventh of thirteen children.

In many ways, Jesse's childhood was idyllic, but one frustration kept blocking his way. His parents and pastor expressed no concern for his spiritual wellbeing. Many evenings Jesse lay on the floor with a large picture Bible, but no one told him the stories. He later recalled, "I asked my mother especially many, many questions until she lost patience with me.... Usually the answer was, 'You are not old enough to understand that.'"[34]

Jesse grew so burdened he couldn't sleep or eat, and in desperation he again approached his mother, begging her to let him join the church. Her reply stayed with him for years: "Son, you are too young." This answer had a devastating effect. Jesse later recalled how his attitude changed: "Well, I'm lost and I can't get saved now. I can't get any more lost, so I guess I'll just sin if I want to."

> "I asked my mother especially many, many questions until she lost patience with me.... Usually the answer was, 'You are not old enough to understand that.'"

He began hanging around the pool halls, gambling, cussing, and drinking. He later said the years between the ages of 12 and 20 were "full of dark memories" for him, accompanied by periodic whippings. Jesse ran away from home when he was 18 and found work doing hard manual labor. His mother, whose health was failing, discovered renewed spiritual vitality after reading Hannah Whitall Smith's classic, *The Christian's Secret of a Happy Life*. She began praying for Jesse and writing to him. Then one of Jesse's brothers, Derius, trusted Christ as his personal Savior, and he soon persuaded his parents to have a daily time of family prayer and Bible reading. The Overholtzers drew closer as a family as they gathered nightly to pray, especially for Jesse.

Maria eventually persuaded her husband to look for their wayward son. Sam found Jesse in a cheap boarding house and offered to send him to college if he'd return home. Jesse eventually agreed and enrolled in Lordsburg College in La Verne, California. During his first year at Lordsburg, a series of evangelistic meetings was held in the chapel. Jesse agreed to attend just one service. That evening every sentence seemed aimed at the young prodigal, and at the invitation Jesse was the first to respond. "I was such a sinner that I came 'all of grace' and threw myself on the mercy of God," he later said. "I not only accepted Jesus as my personal Savior but surrendered my life to Him as best I knew."[35]

Maria lived just long enough to see the answer to her prayers. Soon after her death and while he was still in college, Jesse married Anna M. Ewing and began establishing a Christian home and making a living. A 1901 entry in a California biographical record reported: "In a list of rising young businessmen of Lordsburg the name of Mr. (Jesse Irvin) Overholtzer should be given. The success that he has attained proves his possession of more than ordinary ability.... For one year after leaving college Mr. Overholtzer was proprietor and publisher of the Lordsburg Sunbeam, which he founded and which was published weekly. At this writing he acts as local agent for the Hartford Fire Insurance Company, and is also a part owner of the Lordsburg Water Company's Plant."[36]

But Overholtzer's heart was quickly moving toward a different vocation. He wasn't satisfied publishing the news and overseeing the water company. He wanted to share the Good News and offer the water of life to those who were thirsty. He began preaching as opportunities arose, for he felt God was calling him to enter the ministry.

That's when his problems began.

CHAPTER 2

The Ministry Years

J ESSE ENTERED THE MINISTRY IN A DENOMINATION THAT WAS LEGALISTIC AND OPPRESSIVE. People were expelled from church if they installed carpet in their homes. Women were excluded if they wore hats instead of bonnets. Men wore beards, and photographs were eschewed. Jesse regularly preached two or three times a week while still farming. But his message was one of salvation by works, the essential theology of his denomination, which he later summarized as "beards, bonnets, and buggies."[37] His ministry bore little fruit, and he began doubting his own salvation.

One day as he passed a particular shop, he saw a box of used books and offered to buy the lot of them for 25 cents. Among them was a biography of evangelist D. L. Moody, a man whom Jesse had criticized. In reading Moody's story, Jesse saw a fire and a faith he himself lacked. "It became clear to me that Mr. Moody taught salvation by grace, and at last I began to search the Scriptures to see if it could be possible that my teaching had been wrong. I literally discovered the word 'grace' in my Bible."

He longed to launch into a thorough Bible study to determine whether the Bible taught salvation by works or by grace, but he didn't have the time. Between farming and pastoring, he was busy from morning to night. Then scarlet fever struck and Jesse was confined to his house for 13 weeks. With nothing else to do, he undertook a complete re-study of the Bible. "I asked the Lord for His guidance as I began the study and promised Him that I would follow the truth as I found it, regardless of the cost." He made a list of the passages that spoke of grace, another list of the passages that taught salvation was not by works, and another list of the passages that made it clear salvation was based on faith in Christ's crucifixion and resurrection. Jesse memorized many of the Bible's key texts about grace.

During his 1914 quarantine, he gained enough strength to tend to the trees in his peach orchard. "I spent my days pruning trees and my evenings poring over the Book while the inward battle went on," he wrote. "From the top of my high ladder, I went over every text in my mind.... As this avalanche of truth filled my mind more and more, I said to myself, 'It must be so, it must be so.' Then I said, 'It is so.' Finally I said, 'I accept it for myself.' At that instant the Holy Spirit flooded my soul with His sweet presence and from that moment to the present I have been conscious of His presence in my heart, in varying degrees, every waking moment."[38]

Running to the house, he shared his experience with his wife, who also embraced salvation by grace. When the quarantine lifted, Jesse began preaching "grace" at church. He shaved off his beard and gave a new face to his new faith. The congregation grew and soon had to move their services to the local school auditorium. He purchased an automobile to visit more widely, and many people professed Christ as their Savior. He encountered denominational resistance, but he persevered, even when his initial enthusiasm gave way to the stress and strain of shepherding a diverse group of adults.

Meanwhile, Jesse purchased a 24-volume set of Charles H. Spurgeon's sermons, and while reading it came across this sentence: "A child of five, if properly instructed, can as readily believe and be regenerated as anyone."

> **"A child of five, if properly instructed, can as readily believe and be regenerated as anyone."**

Here was a new challenge. Just as Jesse's background had been seeped with a legalism that took years to overcome, it had also been influenced by a belief that children are not old enough to make spiritual decisions. He felt Spurgeon was wrong, but the question nagged at him. Finally, he took an opportunity to speak to several children from non-Christian homes who were attending his church. To his astonishment, about 20 of them received Christ as their Savior.

Two of the children were sisters, age 9 and 11, from a home where the father was an infidel and the mother hadn't been to church for years. Shortly afterward, the mother came to Christ too, saying she had been convinced of the truth of the Gospel by "the changed lives of my two little girls."

This was in 1916, and Jesse became gripped by the cause of child evangelism. After nearly suffering a breakdown during the flu epidemic of 1918, Jesse withdrew from his denomination, gave up his ordination credentials, and relocated his family to Berkeley, California. In 1919, they moved into the house at 2119 Carleton Street, about a mile from the University of California.

Soon Jesse was leading Bible classes throughout the Bay area, including a college-age class attended by 100 college students.

He and his fellow missionaries secured the use of churches near public school buildings and conducted children's Bible classes. Two young ladies from the Bible Institute of Los Angeles (BIOLA, now Biola University) were hired to help oversee the work. At the close of the first month, 300 children had professed Jesus Christ as their Lord and Savior. Jesse began training more missionaries in leading children to Christ, and soon nearly every evangelical church in the Bay Area was hosting children's meetings.

In some areas, however, there was no suitable church building near a school. In such cases, Jesse secured safe, private homes. He soon saw that Bible clubs in homes were better attended than those in churches, and eventually most of the meetings were held in homes. They were called Home Bible Classes, Neighborhood Bible Classes, Bible Clubs, Good News Clubs, and the like.[39]

The work grew rapidly as children were evangelized and discipled. Yet all the while, Jesse was using up his savings. One day he ransacked his pockets to realize he had only 35 cents to his name. While pondering his dilemma, a friend called and asked to meet him at San Francisco's Palace Hotel, a bus trip that required a 35-cent fare. Arriving at the hotel penniless, Jesse was stunned when his friend, who knew nothing of his financial needs, gave him $1,000 to help with his work.

> **Jesse was stunned when his friend, who knew nothing of his financial needs, gave him $1,000 to help with his work.**

Bolstered by such experiences and knowing an organizational structure was necessary to oversee the expanding ministry, Jesse founded the Christian Training Association (the forerunner of Child Evangelism Fellowship) on March 23, 1922, with a board of directors made up of area church leaders and with Jesse serving as the director. Soon Children's Home Bible Classes were being launched in cities throughout California, and full-time child evangelism missionaries were recruited and hired. In 1923, a six-month school was started to train children's missionaries, with 15 graduates the first year. Each month, the statistics for the home groups grew. In October of 1924, for example, 559 children professed Christ as their Savior.

That year, Jesse began a monthly magazine entitled *The Week Day Bible School World*. The next year, open-air child evangelism rallies began in Sacramento. In the innocence of those times, few people questioned children's missionaries who stood near the entrances of public schools at closing time and gathered a crowd of students with whom they freely shared the Word of Life. As Jesse drove up and down the West Coast—from California to Washington—he prayed for the children of every town he passed, asking the Lord to give them an opportunity to hear the Gospel.

In time, Jesse felt the tug eastward toward Chicago. In June of 1933, he arrived by rail with hardly any money and nowhere to live. He was 56 years old and alone, for his family had to remain in California. By mid-July, he found living quarters but was down to his last 26 cents. "I traveled on a shoestring," he recalled, "but God was in the shoestring."[40]

His attempts to begin training classes were just marginally successful, and only his passionate love for child evangelism sustained him as he took to the streets trying to establish works in resistant neighborhoods. He devoted the entire summer of 1934 to witnessing for Christ in open-air evangelism in neighborhoods all over town.

TEN WEEKS IN CHICAGO

In the summer of 1934, I spent ten weeks on open-air child evangelism in the congested sections of Chicago. One afternoon, soon after I began my work, I came to a group of 12 boys. A hydrant had broken, the street was flooded, and they were playing in the water with improvised boats. At first they were too intent on their play to stop to see The Wordless Book, which I offered to show them. Suddenly I had unexpected help. It developed that four of these boys had been led to Christ on a visit I had made to that neighborhood about a month earlier, but I did not recognize any of them. These four began to urge the other boys to give up their play and listen to what I had to tell them.

This they finally did, and they gathered closely around me as I told them the Story of Stories. Then each one was led to accept the Lord as his own Savior....

All the boys but one went back to their play. Dickson, seven years of age, followed me. He soon discovered that I had two Wordless Books with me, and he asked if he might hold one. As I would turn the pages and explain the colors to group after group of boys and girls, he would turn his pages too, and soon I found he was trying to repeat what I was saying. Soon he said, "I want to help you. I will bring the children to you while you talk to them." This he did, with the greatest faithfulness and success....

In those days I kept a careful book account of my open-air work. My records show that during that afternoon 88 professed to accept Christ—86 children and two young people. Of these children, 56 were boys and 30 were girls. During the afternoon I found nine who had accepted Christ on my former visit, and seven children who utterly refused to accept the Savior—one of them said I was crazy.[41]

Jesse Overholtzer

One particular Sunday, Overholtzer was down to his last two cents. That wasn't enough to ride to Moody Church as had been his habit, so he attended a church in his neighborhood. When the collection plate passed, he put his two pennies into the offering. The next day's mail brought sufficient funding to continue the work.

While in Chicago, Jesse abandoned a handful of minor theological errors that had kept many Christian leaders at a distance from him. His doctrines became sounder through diligent study of Scripture, and he worked hard to convince church leaders of the need to emphasize child evangelism. His prayer life deepened, and he came to accept and experience the "Victorious Christian Life" as he read the writings of the Sunday school publisher H. Clay Trumbull.

"One day as I was praying," Jesse recalled, "the spirit of prayer came upon me as I had never known it. While fully conscious, I seemed to lose the sense of time or place. For hours I literally lay on the floor on my face and wept as the Spirit compelled me to pray for the salvation of children. In great agony I was led to pray from country to country for the children of that country. This continued until I had covered all the countries of the world except Russia. I was just as burdened to pray for the children of Russia but could not bring myself to pray for them. Then the burden lifted.

"About three weeks later this experience was repeated. Again I prayed for the children, country by country, until I came to Russia. I felt I must pray for the children of that great country. In fact it seemed that I would die if I did not. Yet the agony was so great it seemed that I would die if I did pray for them. I told the Lord I was willing to die then and there if He would give me the strength and faith to pray for the salvation of Russia's children. He gave me enabling grace and the prayer was uttered; then the burden lifted."[42]

One of the interesting aspects of this stage in Overholtzer's life was his propensity to weeping. "I was overwhelmed by the spirit of weeping," he later wrote. "The weeping was beyond my control. As I prayed, I wept and wept. The uncontrollable weeping has been experienced hundreds of times since in prayer and many, many times in public addresses as I presented child evangelism and the spiritual plight of America's childhood. I cannot sit in an audience where reports of children being saved are presented without weeping beyond my control. It would seem that this weeping is wholly of the Holy Spirit. At least I have no other explanation for it. My efforts to control it are a complete failure."[43]

He became known as the Weeping Prophet. Dr. Frank Mann, who later served as president of CEF, said, "I can still visualize him standing before the audience as he emceed the meetings and when he would begin to talk about the children he would break down in tears. Someone else would step forward and emcee until he had his tears under control. I saw this happen time and time again."[44]

Jesse Overholtzer was now in the grip of deep conviction that God had called him to catalyze a mighty work for the salvation of children. "By the very nature of the call which the Lord gave me, it became crystal clear that God was going to do a mighty work for the salvation of children in these last days," he wrote. "The fact that there was a supernatural prayer burden for the children of every land indicated that this blessing was to become worldwide. No such prominence or scope for a work primarily for children had ever been known."[45]

In 1935, Jesse formed a committee that met in the office of Gwendolin C. Armour (wife of Philip Armour, the head of the Armour meatpacking company) on the 19th floor of 203 N. Wabash Avenue in Chicago. With much prayer, the group devised plans for reaching the children of Chicago with Bible clubs. When Overholtzer felt the organization in Chicago was self-sustaining, he boarded the train for California, stopping along the way in Albuquerque to start a child evangelism committee there.

In Los Angeles, a group of missionaries met to organize a committee there, and the price of the noonday luncheon was 25 cents. On the way, Overholtzer, who was penniless, saw a quarter in the gutter, picked it up, and went on his way rejoicing.

These organizational building blocks in California, New Mexico, Chicago, and elsewhere became the foundation stones of Child Evangelism Fellowship. But what was lacking was an overarching organization that would bring unity to all the parts and provide a national framework for expansion. Overholtzer felt that Dr. Paul Rood, the President of Biola, was the man to lead such an organization. Rood initially declined. But then he learned that Jesse Overholtzer had spent the last three days without food or money before receiving a check for $100 from a supporter in Chicago. "If one man could so gladly sacrifice himself for the sake of child evangelism," Rood thought, "I can sacrifice my time."

Rood agreed to become the president of the committee with Overholtzer directing the work, and the National Child Evangelism Committee was launched in Rood's office at the Bible Institute of Los Angeles on November 1, 1935.[46]

The peppery Irish revivalist, Dr. J. Edwin Orr, was in Los Angeles at the time and was enthralled with Overholtzer and his passion. Orr noticed that Overholtzer was always close to tears because of two things—a burden for the salvation of children and his frustration with the difficulties in getting his work to children started. Orr was amazed at American indifference to child evangelism, for in Great Britain it had been a major initiative since the 1859 revival and the leadership of E. Payson Hammond.

It was Orr who contributed a title and a slogan to the cause. Overholtzer was going to call his organization "The Child Evangelism Missionary Society," but Orr suggested he use the word "Fellowship" in order to be more interdenominational and inclusive. Hence, we're known to this day as Child Evangelism Fellowship. Orr also coined the movement's first slogan: "Capture the Children for Christ."[47]

"If I had my life to live over," explained Rood as CEF came into being, "I would devote it to child evangelism. If I deal with 20 adults, I am usually able to win one to Christ; but if I deal with 20 children, 19 of them will accept Christ. The next great revival will be a children's revival."[48]

> ## The next great revival will be a children's revival." -Dr. Paul Rood

In 1936, Jesse and Maria Overholtzer traveled from city to city establishing local CEF works, but often with little funding. In Omaha, Overholtzer pawned his overcoat in the dead of winter for money to buy a meal and a ticket to the next city. Evangelism projects began dotting the map: Denver, Salt Lake City, Omaha, Des Moines, Kansas City, St. Louis, Indianapolis, Louisville, Cincinnati, Philadelphia, Baltimore, Washington, and more.

The Overholtzers rode trains and buses from city to city, living frugally, calling on church leaders and Christian professionals, setting up CEF committees in every city where they could find a foothold.

Child Evangelism Fellowship was incorporated as a national movement in Chicago on May 20, 1937, with its headquarters in Mrs. Armour's offices in Chicago's Loop. Mrs. Armour donated more than her offices; she oversaw the local works in Chicago. Leaving her home in Lake Forest, she would direct her chauffeur to an area on the south side of town, exit her vehicle, walk into the neighborhoods, and talk to the children in groups. She led many to Christ as her chauffeur waited a few streets away.[49]

When ill health forced Mrs. Overholtzer to return to California, her husband traveled on alone. While Jesse was in

Wichita, Kansas, in April of 1938, news came that his wife had taken a turn for the worse. He left immediately for California, but she suffered a fatal heart attack before he could reach Los Angeles. His children, by then all married with families of their own, gathered with him to mourn their loss. Immediately after the funeral, Jesse returned to Kansas and continued his travels.

"I seemed to be driven by the Holy Spirit to visit every city in the United States and Canada in the least possible time, staying only long enough to lay a burden of the evangelization of children upon the hearts of the Lord's people," he wrote. "In nearly every place I visited, a CEF organization, however small, was formed."[50]

When trains and buses proved ineffective for getting to second-tier cities, Overholtzer purchased an automobile. As Christian publications popularized the CEF movement, he was able to secure speaking engagements more easily, and doors began opening in churches, conference centers, Bible institutes, and Christian colleges. "In all these public addresses the Lord limited me to one message—that of child evangelism and the responsibility of the Lord's people to evangelize the children in their homes, in their Sunday schools, in their cities, states, and in the whole nation."[51]

Overholtzer so often preached from Matthew 18 about reaching children for Christ that the words rubbed off that page in his Bible and eventually the page itself wore out. But as he and his Bible wore out, the work increased exponentially and children across America heard the Good News.

CHAPTER 3

The Miracle Years

As JESSE OVERHOLTZER CRISSCROSSED THE UNITED STATES, ANOTHER BURDEN GREW ON HIS HEART; THE POSSIBILITY OF ORGANIZING EVANGELISTIC EFFORTS FOR CHILDREN IN OTHER REGIONS OF THE WORLD. He mentioned this burden in his talks, but his responsibilities were so great in the United States that he couldn't imagine how the work could be expanded internationally. One man wrote him, saying, "I think the idea of going to the mission fields is crazy, but here is a $100 check to help finance it."[52]

In March of 1939, Jesse aimed his car south and crossed the border into Mexico, organizing CEF chapters all the way to Mexico City. Then for the first time, he took to the air, flying by Pan-American Airways to Guatemala, Salvador, Honduras, Nicaragua, and Costa Rica. CEF gained a toehold in each of these countries and thereby became an international ministry.

On May 4, 1939, after returning from Mexico and Central America, Jesse married Ruth Pennebaker, an Oregon native, Biola graduate, and avid CEF missionary. The couple settled into a modest home in San Antonio and began planning a trip through the Caribbean region and Latin America to recruit and train CEF missionaries, and organize the work there. On Christmas afternoon, with Mr. Overholtzer recovering from surgery on his foot, they traveled by train from San Antonio to Miami, then by air to Cuba.

For three months, the Overholtzers organized work in Cuba, Jamaica, Panama, Columbia, Ecuador, Peru, Bolivia, Chile, Argentina, Brazil, and Venezuela. They depended on checks forwarded from the Chicago office and were often down to pennies. Ruth suffered dysentery, and the rigors of travel wore both of them down. But the seed so intensively planted in those days still flourishes today.

The first CEF full-time overseas missionaries were appointed in 1941—Mr. and Mrs. Harry Briault, who served in Brazil. The following years saw the number increase to three, then six, then nine.[53]

Back in Texas, Jesse and Ruth were squeezing some orange juice for breakfast on December 7, 1941, when they were stunned to hear radio reports of the attack on Pearl Harbor. World War II disrupted Jesse's plans to travel to Africa, where he had hoped to begin CEF works. So he gave himself to answering correspondence from his home in Texas and writing study books for teacher training classes. Ruth compiled a volume of *Salvation Songs for Children* and *Our Daily Bread* booklets for children to use in their daily devotions.

Then Jesse had another idea—starting a magazine to represent Child Evangelism Fellowship. Ruth was skeptical of launching such a venture in wartime. His response was, "We're in a war too, an invisible war, a struggle for children's souls; and a magazine will be ammunition." Ruth prayerfully acquiesced.

With the help of Dallas Seminary graduate students, the first issue of *Child Evangelism* magazine appeared in March of 1942.[54]

Another initiative was developing Bible lessons for the Good News Clubs, which were meeting weekly throughout North and South America. That became Ruth's project. At first she was overwhelmed by the thought of providing weekly lessons for thousands of children. But one night while very ill, the great doctrines of the Bible she had studied under Dr. R. A. Torrey began forming themselves into simple lessons, and the ideas came to her in torrents. She later said, "I spent the next 15 years working out a series of lessons which had been given to me in embryonic form that night in San Antonio."[55]

The first CEF Bible stories included cardboard illustrations that were cut out and fastened to wooden spools to make them stand up. Then one day, Overholtzer was talking to a friend who shared an idea. This man's daughter, playing in the backyard near the clothesline, had thrown her nightgown against the flannel sheet—it stuck! She called her father to reach up and pull it off. The man, intrigued, began experimenting with the way flannel stuck to flannel. He showed Overholtzer some of his projects, and soon Overholtzer was standing in front of his CEF staff, giving a demonstration. "As he was talking," someone recalled, "he took a square board, covered it with flannel, put it against a desk and placed about five figures on it. They stayed on. We were amazed."[56] The first "flannelgraph" series, *The Bible, the Word of God* was released in 1945.

ONE FLANNELGRAPH BOARD

I grew up in Long Beach, California, where my mother was a psychology major from UCLA and believed Christianity was superstition. My father was a chemical engineer and a humanist. I had two sisters and a little brother, Keith. A next door neighbor named Mrs. Blakely opened her backyard for a CEF Bible study and all four of us children received Christ. My mother was also saved, then my dad—our whole family! My brother Keith joined Wycliffe Bible Translators, investing his life to working in four language groups in Cameroon. I've been faithful in church as a choir member and prayer warrior. When you calculate the chain reactions taking place, it's amazing to think what God can do with one flannelgraph board.

David Bevin

Having studied other child evangelism movements of the past, Overholtzer grew concerned that CEF needed a means of training its missionaries around the world. On January 2, 1945, at the height of the war, Mr. Overholtzer and several coworkers at the Dallas Seminary and the nearby Scofield Memorial Church began the Child Evangelism Institute with 30 students from 14 states, 2 Canadian provinces, and the nation of Ecuador.

In the opening session, Overholtzer said, "We are going to have this Institute tremendously big someday by the grace of God. Many others will be patterned after it over the whole world. Great Britain has already written asking how to start one.... I think this is just an inkling of what is coming, for teacher training is at the heart of the movement. When the Lord began leading me out into this ministry I couldn't find a Sunday school teacher who knew how to lead a soul to Christ, and I knew a lot of them. Some were in good churches. If we were ever going to do anything in child evangelism, we had to train teachers..."

Overholtzer continued, "The Savior had a world vision. He said, 'Go into all the world... and preach the Gospel to every creature.' That is the kind of vision Jesus had, and He has never changed. We should get the same kind of vision. I am foolish enough to believe that when Jesus said every creature He included the children. After I came to see that children could be evangelized," he told the students, "I was able to win 100 souls where I won one before without working any harder."[57]

> **"After I came to see that children could be evangelized," he told the students, "I was able to win 100 souls where I won one before without working any harder."**

Six months later, the first graduating class marched across the platform of Scofield Memorial Church, after hearing Dr. John F. Walvoord speak on the topic: "Why Preach to Children." The next year, 37 students showed up. This institute, which continues today, has been the backbone for the trained leadership needed by CEF. One participant called it the "West Point" for winning children.[58]

During these days, Jesse's health deteriorated. When it became clear the Texas heat was taking its toll, Jesse and Ruth decided to move to California to be near family and friends. Relocating was difficult during the war, but the Lord provided a home in Pacific Palisades in the Los Angeles area. So in the mid-1940s, the administrative offices, the Chicago literature depot, Child Evangelism Institute, and *Child Evangelism* magazine were all consolidated and brought to Pacific Palisades, where the Overholtzers settled down and began planning for an annual conference for their global team of children's evangelists.

Meanwhile, CEF chapters were expanding overseas—India and Argentina in 1947, Japan and Burma in 1948, Australia in 1949, Taiwan and Tonga in 1951, the Philippines in 1952, Fiji in 1953.[59] On April 28-30, 1947, the first Child Evangelism Conference convened at Moody Memorial Church in Chicago. A second conference was held in Philadelphia in 1948; a third at Bob Jones University in 1949; and a fourth at Biola in 1950.

Overholtzer retired from the work in 1952 at age 75, though he continued to teach at the Institute, visit the chapel services, write columns for the magazine, and pray earnestly for the work. "If you don't think God can use you," he told students, "look at me. See what God did with a nobody. He'll use you too if you keep fully yielded to Him and trust Him to work through you."[60]

Living only two blocks from the CEF headquarters allowed Jesse to continue teaching in the institute right up to the week of his death. On August 4, 1955, he suffered a crippling heart attack and passed away two days later at age 78. By the time of Jesse Overholtzer's death, CEF had chapters in more than 1,000 American cities and 60 other countries.[61]

Dr. Paul Rood, learning of Overholtzer's death, wrote, "His vision was the evangelization of the children of the world and his passion was their salvation. No man has had such a vision and the plan for carrying it out. Probably from the standpoint of eternity, Child Evangelism Fellowship was and is the greatest movement of the 20th century. Brother Overholtzer was the father of this movement."[62]

CHAPTER 4

The Middle Years

F JESSE OVERHOLTZER WAS THE FATHER OF CHILD EVANGELISM FELLOWSHIP, HERBERT J. Taylor became the captain of the ship and helped steer the ministry after Overholtzer's death. As chairman of the Board of CEF, Taylor put the organization on a firm financial and organizational footing. Taylor's story is as impressive as Overholtzer's and serves as the prelude to the opportunity God would give another manufacturer named Reese Kauffman, who, a generation later, would assume leadership of the ministry.

Herb Taylor was born in 1893 in Michigan's Upper Peninsula. His father was a businessman who instilled in his children an entrepreneurial spirit. When Herb was 16, he attended a revival meeting at a Methodist church and responded to the invitation to receive Christ as his Savior. He went on to study at Northwestern University in Chicago; where even as a college student he managed himself with discipline and maturity. "I carried a notebook and scheduled every hour of every day for a week in advance," he said. "The schedule allowed an average of about six hours sleep a night, but I stuck to it."[63]

Taylor returned home after serving in the Navy during World War I to marry his sweetheart and decide what to do with his life.

He had two job offers. One was with the Young Men's Christian Association, a position with more ministry potential than financial promise. The other was with the Sinclair Oil Company. Taylor sought the advice of his friend, George Perkins, an associate of financier J. P. Morgan. Perkins told him to go into business and become so successful that by age 45 he would be wealthy enough to devote his time to working with young people for the cause of Christ.

"Mr. Perkins was the vehicle through which I'm certain God presented me with a plan—his particular plan for me. No man could have predicted my life with such accuracy.... From the moment I left Mr. Perkin's office, I knew the course of my life. It was one of the most confident and wonderful moments in my life."[64]

After moving to Oklahoma, Taylor became a rising star at Sinclair Oil. His gifted personality made him a natural salesman, and his organizational skills enabled him to be effective with everything he did. In 1924, Taylor was recruited as an executive for the Jewel Tea Company, and he relocated to Chicago. There his career advanced quickly, and by 1930 he was in line to become president.

All the while, Taylor was cultivating his spiritual life. He diligently studied the Bible every day and worked hard on Scripture memory. He and his wife taught a Sunday school class for teens at their local church.

When the stock market crashed, the Great Depression endangered many companies. One of them was Club Aluminum Utensil Company, which sold waterless cookware. Taylor took over the company and managed to turn it around. By the late 1930s, Taylor had achieved a level of financial and vocational success that, as anticipated, allowed him to devote himself and his income to Christian work. He was especially drawn to ministries aimed at young people. He was instrumental in helping launch InterVarsity Christian Fellowship and the Urbana Missionary Conference. Taylor was also involved in forming Fuller Theological Seminary, Youth for Christ, and Young Life. He was the driving force behind Pioneer Girls and Christian Service Brigade. Taylor also helped promote Christian broadcasting in Chicago and recruited a young soloist named George Beverly Shea for his radio program, which paved the way for Shea to become associated with Billy Graham. It was also Taylor who brought organizational structure and increased financial backing for the Billy Graham crusades.

But Taylor felt one thing was still lacking—a ministry to effectively evangelize elementary-age children. Mrs. Philip Armour, who knew both Overholtzer and Taylor, determined to bring the two men together. On April 7, 1944, Mrs. Armour wrote to Jesse, "My dear Mr. Overholtzer: Mr. Herbert J. Taylor, about whom I have written you before, asked me to write you to tell you that he will be in Dallas on April 27 and would like to see you.... Mr. Taylor is an excellent businessman and would also give us a steer through his interest and through his proposed 'man' in running our chapters in a more businesslike way. I feel sure a talk between you two would lead to great things for the children of the United States."[65]

Taylor described the events in his memoir, saying:

> The late Mrs. Phillip Armour—wife of an Armour
> & Company Meat Packers executive—was a member
> of our InterVarsity Christian Fellowship Board. Every

time we held a meeting, somehow she managed to twist the conversation around and direct my thoughts toward a certain J. Irvin Overholtzer on the West Coast. Mr. Overholtzer had started some clubs on the West Coast specifically for the purpose of reaching the unchurched among the very young.

Finally, Mrs. Armour convinced me I should... have a talk with Mr. Overholtzer. Child evangelism was close to my heart—it represented the one unfulfilled part of our God-given plan. When Mrs. Armour pointed out that what Mr. Overholtzer really needed was organizational ability, someone who could synchronize the work of his clubs on a national and international basis, the die was cast and out I went.

As soon as I talked with Mr. Overholtzer, I knew that God had filled in the plan for me, and soon after my return to Chicago, we did what was necessary to organize "National Child Evangelism Fellowship," with Mr. Overholtzer's approval.

During this time, Taylor developed a serious illness and was confined to bed for many days. He used his time to memorize the Sermon on the Mount and determined to absorb this passage into his thinking and actions. From that point in 1947 to the end of his life, Taylor recited the Sermon on the Mount to himself word-for-word every day. He later wrote, "In those beautiful words is the formula for peace, for brotherhood, and for all the fine things for which men have yearned since the dawn of creation."[66]

Recovering, Herbert J. Taylor guided the Board and helped infuse CEF with funds. But he never served as president.

Franklin F. Ellis was appointed international director when Mr. Overholtzer retired. He oversaw the ministry until 1959.

From 1959 to 1961, James S. Kiefer led CEF. Under his leadership CEF moved its headquarters from Pacific Palisades to Grand Rapids. During Kiefer's tenure, CEF published the first 5-Day Club teaching materials.[67]

Jacob DeBruin led CEF from 1962 to 1965, launching a new era of growth as Child Evangelism Fellowship expanded rapidly across Europe, with zealous missionaries like Sam Doherty of Northern Ireland fanning the flame. In his book *A Life Worth Living*, Sam recalled his first attempt at child evangelism. He took his flannelboard and easel to a housing estate near his home in Northern Ireland and invited children to come. Between 30 and 40 children showed up every day. Doherty presented the Gospel as clearly as he could, but none of the children showed any interest. By the end of the week, Doherty was tired and disappointed.

Years later, he returned to the same town to speak at a local church. One of the leaders invited him to lunch, and the man lived in the very housing estate where Doherty had made his seemingly futile attempt at child evangelism. Over lunch the man described one of his neighbors, a young lady who had recently died of leukemia. Doherty asked if she had been a Christian.

"Yes, she was a fine Christian," said the man, who went on to explain that years before someone had come to the estate every morning for five days and conducted meetings for the children. "This little girl was sick and couldn't attend the meetings, but she asked her mother to open the window so she could hear what the man was saying. During the week as she lay in her bed she trusted the Lord Jesus as her Savior. Since that day she grew in the Lord and in her faith. Isn't that a wonderful story?"

"You have no idea how wonderful it is," replied Sam. "I was that man and I was so disappointed that nothing had happened that week!"[68]

In this way, the Gospel began spreading child to child, nation to nation as Child Evangelism Fellowship spread around the world.

AND IN AFRICA

Stephen Rutuna, a young diplomat in Burundi, lived in the capital of Bujumbura with his wife and three children. His governmental career was thriving, and he rose to the position of Prime Minister. But after a life-changing encounter with Jesus Christ, Stephen felt God calling him to work with children. He told the king he would serve one more year before resigning office to fully devote himself to child evangelism. But at the end of the year, the king threatened to have Stephen killed if he left his position. When Stephen refused, he was imprisoned and condemned to death by dismemberment. But when the moment came for Stephen to be killed, a furious storm arose. A bolt of lightning struck the ground near him, and Stephen was knocked unconscious. When he came to, he heard the soldiers discussing what to do. "We cannot kill this man!" they said. "His God has done this and is more powerful. We are afraid to touch him."

The king agreed. But when Stephen returned home, he found his house burned to the ground and his family missing. As it turned out, local CEF missionaries in Burundi had rescued and sheltered the Rutuna family and Stephen was shortly reunited with them. For several months the CEF missionaries hid the family until they were able to escape to Uganda, where Stephen began the CEF work in that nation. When Idi Amin rose to power, the Rutunas again had to flee. This time they settled in Kenya, where Stephen became the first national director for CEF work there. He later served as regional director for East and Central Africa, a position he filled until his retirement. Stephen labored faithfully for the souls of boys and girls until the Lord took him to Heaven.[69]

The Gospel spread through a growing global network of children's missionaries, with progress on several fronts. In Denmark, for example, Minnie Larsen faced resistance when she first arrived to establish a work there for CEF. The country was in ruins from the devastation of World War II. People were shell-shocked, hungry, cold, and wary of strangers in their country. When Minnie showed someone her Gospel tract for children, the reply was, "If this is what you're going to talk about in Denmark, you might as well go home."

She stayed, of course, and three months later managed to secure a display booth at the World Baptist Congress meeting in Copenhagen. While she set up her materials, a seven-year-old boy came by. He paused to look, intrigued by the flannelgraph pictures. Seizing the opportunity, Minnie asked, "Would you like to hear a story?"

He replied, "If it's about the Bible, I don't want to hear it!"

Although taken aback, Minnie persevered. Pulling out her *Wordless Book*, she began taking him through the colors as she explained the plan of salvation. Every page drew him in, and when she got to the wonderful news that we can have a relationship with God and eternal life through the love of Jesus Christ, the boy broke down and cried. That youngster became Minnie's first token of fruitfulness in Denmark, and by the end of the conference he had brought a number of other children to talk with Minnie, all of whom trusted Christ as Savior. That was the beginning of CEF evangelism work in war-torn Denmark.[70]

...the Gospel penetrated the Iron Curtain in remarkable ways.

As CEF swept across Europe following the war, the Gospel penetrated the Iron Curtain in remarkable ways. One Polish youth named Czesław Bassara lived in a Christian family close to the remains of the Nazi concentration camp of Auschwitz. As a young man Czcsław was attracted to Communism and became the leader of the Communist organization in his school. One night he returned home late and overheard his mother praying for him. "Dear God, save my boy and get him out of his way of living."

Czesław angrily interrupted her, shouting, "Stop praying! I will never become a Christian! I choose Communism as my way of life!"

"Czesław, my beloved son," she cried, "you have to remember as long as my heart is beating I will be praying for you!"

Soon after, Czesław's father invited the local church to meet in their newly built house. That meant Christians would meet in Czesław's bedroom! This so enraged the young man that he built a homemade bomb and placed it in the cellar under this bedroom. One evening as the Lord's Supper was served in his room, Czesław detonated the bomb. It damaged the house and the nerves of the worshippers, but no one was killed in the blast. Instead, the church dedicated itself to pray earnestly for Czesław's salvation.

A few months later, Czesław was invited to a Christian camp 600 kilometers (373 miles) from his home in Gdansk. He decided to go, though he later confessed he didn't know why. Night after night he sat through the presentation of the Gospel and it began to grip his heart. One night when the invitation was given, he went forward, not to be saved but to try to understand how the Christians wielded so much influence over young people. An old Polish preacher explained the message of Jesus to the responders, and many were saved. But not Czesław. Yet, in the silence of the moment, the young Communist seemed to hear the Lord telling him: "This is your time. It will never again be given to you." At that moment, Czesław received Christ as his Savior.

He returned home and began attending the church meeting in his home—the congregation he had bombed. Soon he was invited to teach children. He also enrolled in theological studies and later in the CEF Leadership Training Institute at Kilchzimmer, Switzerland. Czesław and his wife Helena began organizing children's camps, training courses and children's missionary conferences in Poland and became leaders of the work behind the Iron Curtain and in post-Communist Europe. They're still active today in the work of CEF, as are their children, Bogdan and Dorota.[71]

The rapid and sustained growth of child evangelism around the world posed organizational challenges to CEF leadership.

Dr. Frank Mann, a chiropractor who had been involved with CEF for 24 years, became executive director. Under Mann's years at the helm, the total number of children reached worldwide was nearly two million, and there was a significant increase in full-time overseas national missionaries.[72] In 1968, the Here's How radio program began airing, hosted by Rev. Alan George, and in 1970, CEF launched its first television program, The Treehouse Club.

QUICK DRAW SAM

Sam Butcher, the artist behind the popular Precious Moments drawings and figurines, got something of a start while working at Child Evangelism Fellowship when CEF Headquarters was in Grand Rapids. He worked in the shipping department and often drew figures and pictures on the packages being sent out. Because of this he became a CEF artist. When CEF began The Treehouse Club, Sam agreed to appear on the show as Quick Draw Sam, illustrating CEF lessons on the chalkboard. One day, Quick Draw told the children viewing the telecast: "Come up close to the TV. I want to whisper something really special." Then he proceeded to explain how Jesus died for their sins and rose again. If they put their trust in Him, He would become their Savior.

Years later, Sam met a man named Louie and in the course of the conversation asked him how he had become a Christian. Louie explained that as a boy he was often left at home by himself and had watched a television program featuring a character named Quick Draw Sam. One day Quick Draw told the viewers to come close to the television set to hear something special. Louie had walked up to the TV and listened intently. That day he received Christ as Savior.

Louie ended his story by saying he had no idea what had happened to Quick Draw. One day the show wasn't on the air anymore and Louie was unable to find it on other channels. He wondered who Quick Draw was and what had happened to him.

Sam quietly said, "You're looking at him."

Roland R. Gerdes, a New Hampshire pastor and CEF missionary, was appointed president of CEF in July of 1971. By then the work had grown to over 650 salaried directors in North America and over 351 missionaries serving in 67 countries. Christian Youth In Action programs began that year to train young people to teach children, and CEF literature was available in 45 languages by 1975.[73]

In 1975, Gerdes learned of a 668-acre site for sale in Warrenton, Missouri—an abandoned campus owned by the Roman Catholic priesthood of the Passionate Fathers. The Board purchased the property, which included a main building, a set of dormitory-style quarters, a conference center, garages, houses, tennis courts, baseball diamonds, a pavilion and a swimming pool—all in various states of disrepair. The move was controversial. About half of the Grand Rapids staff decided to stay in Michigan. Yet the work pressed onward. In 1976, CEF reported that 609,188 children had been evangelized in the United States alone.[74]

Reidar Kalland served as president from 1977 to 1981, and Ohio native and Navy veteran Alan D. George led CEF from 1981 to 1989. Both bore the heavy burdens of the growing movement. The mortgage on the property in Warrenton, Missouri was fully paid off in 1985, but the property was dilapidated, morale was low, and tension was high. Because CEF chapters had arisen by virtual spontaneous combustion around the world—wherever Mr. Overholtzer or his associates had traveled—the movement lacked centralizing clarity. Herbert Taylor had provided necessary structure for the early days, but he was long gone. As the years passed, the work had fragmented and increasingly the missionaries lacked coordination and cohesion.

That's when God raised up an Indianapolis manufacturer named Reese Kauffman, whose business skills were matched only by his love for the Lord's work. Though he didn't know it at the time, all of his life events had been preparing Reese to step into the arena of child evangelism "for such a time as this." The rest of this book will emphasize the current president of CEF, Reese Kauffman, whose burden is to put CEF ministries into every nation. God has used him in a remarkable way, and our prayer is that you might catch the vision and let God use you to help share the Gospel with all the children of the world.

PART 2

Reese Kauffman and the Mission of Child Evangelism Fellowship

CHAPTER 5
Indelible Influences

EESE KAUFFMAN WAS BORN OCTOBER 27, 1942, IN UNION CITY, PENNSYLVANIA. His father, Rev. Russell Kauffman, pastored a church that started out with only four members. To make a living, Rev. Kauffman traveled and spoke at various functions. He was away from home when Reese was born in Union City's makeshift hospital. His father's absence wasn't a sign of disinterest—the Kauffman household was a loving pastoral home. From childhood, Reese drank in the atmosphere of the church life. Even at an early age he absorbed the mission of evangelism. His first attempt at witnessing happened when he was about two-and-a-half years old. An electrician came to work at the Kauffman house and puffed a cigarette on the front porch. Watching him closely, Reese told him, "If you don't stop 'poking' that cigarette you're going to die and go straight to Hell."

When Reese was three years old, the Kauffmans moved to Indianapolis, Indiana, where Reese's dad took over a church once pastored by the iconic A. W. Tozer. There Reese himself became a Christian at age eight.

When Reese was four years old, he decided his sister Nerus needed to be converted. Having seen people come forward to the altar at church and kneel in tears, he demanded she get down on her knees and start crying. She did kneel, but she couldn't quite make the tears flow. Reese was aggravated by that for he had wanted to tell his parents he had led his sister to the Lord.

From the beginning, Reese had three sets of heroes. The first were his parents. His mother, Neva Kauffman, read the Bible to the children every morning. They never went to school without hearing her read the Bible to them as they ate breakfast. "I recall one time when my dad had to go to the station to catch the fast train to Chicago for a speaking engagement," Reese says. "Mom told us to eat breakfast and wait for her to get back. 'Don't leave for school until I get back,' she warned. She was delayed however, and we began worrying about getting to school on time. We decided to go on to school. Just as we were going up the schoolhouse steps, we heard the honking of a car horn. It was our mom's '54 Chevy. She called us over and scolded us and sat us in the car by the flagpole and read the Scripture to us. I was embarrassed because our friends were all passing us as they went into the building. But I really think my mother had made some kind of vow to God that she would never send her children off to school without reading the Bible to us, and she was determined not to miss a day."

Neva Kauffman had a simple bedtime rule: "Brush your teeth and read your Bible." That became a slogan that stayed with Reese into adulthood and as we'll learn later, led to one of the three greatest days of his life.

The next group of heroes was the missionaries supported by his father and church. "When I was growing up," Reese recalled, "I often gave up my bedroom for missionaries who stayed with us. They regaled me with stories and often gave me artifacts from their fields of service, including headhunter knives and daggers. Those missionaries were heroes to me, with their faraway locations and visionary tasks and warm smiles."

> **"Those missionaries were heroes to me, with their faraway locations and visionary tasks and warm smiles."**

Reese's third group of heroes was the businessmen and businesswomen who attended his dad's church, and he made a point of eavesdropping on their conversations. One man was in the lumber business. Another owned a construction company. Larry Ring was in the plumbing and heating business. Jerry Alderman was a Ford dealer in Indianapolis. Keith Riddle had a restaurant downtown. Reese listened to them talk at church gatherings and social engagements. They were independent, worked for themselves as their own bosses, and were responsible— they cast a long shadow. Reese decided early in life he wanted to be like them—to go into business. From the time he was 14 he wanted to own his own company. But he was torn, because he also wanted to be a missionary. "At the time I couldn't figure out how those two professions could ever come together," he recalls.

The business route opened first and Reese didn't wait long to begin making money. His first enterprise was selling Christmas cards house to house. His dad took him to a wholesaler in downtown Indianapolis, where he purchased cards, ribbons, and wrapping paper. Packing it all in a cardboard box, he hauled it from one door to the next, trying to sell his items to the woman of the house or to whomever opened the door. His initial efforts yielded sparse results. After trying every house in his neighborhood, he begged his dad to drop him off in an adjacent area.

Rev. Kauffman was on his way to church that afternoon, so he left Reese on Central Avenue with a promise to pick him up in an hour and a half. Central Avenue was several miles long, and Reese worked his way doggedly down the street.

Ninety minutes later, his dad found him at the designated corner and asked, "Reese, did you have any success?"

"Dad, I almost sold one!" he said with a grin.

"That was a picture of Reese's optimism," recalled Rev. Kauffman. "He had a work ethic like no one I'd ever met at any age. He was always doing something to make money, and he was always optimistic about everything."

Next, Reese started a lawn mowing business and developed a route of customers. As a teen, he also volunteered to work on local farms so he could drive the tractors. In those days, even youngsters too young to have a driver's license could operate farm equipment on the family property. Reese gladly cleaned out pigpens and pitchforked the muck into the manure spreader just for the joy of driving the tractor and spreading the stuff on the fields. When the farmers saw how hard he worked, they began paying him 50 cents an hour.

In 1959, when Reese was 16 and in high school, he began working for Frank Best, a fellow church member and owner of Best Universal Lock Company. Mr. Best, an inventor at heart, had taught industrial arts at a Seattle high school. One day, he saw students in an adjacent classroom playing with some valuable models. He fumbled with his keys and went through three different sets of locks trying to get into the room to stop them, but it was too late. Some of the models had been damaged. Mr. Best wondered why there wasn't a system of keying that would provide master keys for those needing rapid access to certain rooms for which they were responsible. Mr. Best was a brilliant engineer with several patents to his credit and he went to work on the problem. He perfected locks with interchangeable cores and established Best Lock Company in 1925. He later moved the company to Indianapolis, where the business environment was better. He and his family began attending Rev. Kauffman's church, and a connection was formed with Reese.

"I got a job working the graveyard shift, cleaning the factory restrooms, which got extremely filthy," said Reese. "One night I would clean the men's restroom and the next night I'd clean the women's. My goal was to get those restrooms as clean and shiny as possible by the time people arrived the next morning. I wanted them so clean that someone would notice.

REV. RUSSELL KAUFFMAN'S RECOLLECTIONS

Reese always liked guns. He liked playing cowboy and that sort of thing. He was a great swimmer and learned to water-ski from the back of our boat almost as soon as he knew how to walk. He played football with a team made up from the kids in the neighborhood. When he was in high school, he wanted to buy a motor scooter, so I talked with a good friend of mine who belonged to our church to see if Reese could do some work for him. His name was Frank Best and he owned a company that produced locks.

Mr. Best asked him, "Now, do you really want to work?"

Reese said, "Yeah, I do."

Best gave him a job working from midnight to 8:00 a.m. on Friday and Saturday nights cleaning restrooms. Reese never asked to stay home from church on Sunday morning after working through the night. He just came home, took a shower, and went to church. He was very faithful in all the things he did. Frank recounted to me that sometimes at 4:00 a.m. or so, when he walked through the building, he would find Reese hard at work in one of the restrooms and never goofing off.

During the summers, Reese worked a full 40 hours a week for Best Lock Company. He started as a general laborer on the construction crew, usually shoveling and using the pick. The other men on the crew were making double his wages, but Reese was determined to outwork them. His immediate boss was Herman Bond, a big, burly German who was in charge of maintenance at the Best Lock properties.

One day, as Reese was working on the exterior of the plant, he glanced up at the building and saw something flash by. He caught a glimpse of the same movement a second time, then a third. He finally realized Herman was watching out the window to check on him, to make sure he was working. A day or two later he spotted Herman hiding behind a tree watching him.

"I resolved that Herman would never catch me loafing," said Reese. "Even when the quitting bell rang, I continued working for a minute or two more. I began working as if someone was always watching me, and it became a habit that has persisted all the years since."

Reese's most unusual job at Best Lock came when he was appointed as the company's official fly killer. Mr. Best was opening a new plant. It was a 45,000-square-foot building, plus offices. An open house was planned and customers, employees, and suppliers were coming. The day before the opening, Reese's boss pulled him aside and said, "Reese, there are flies everywhere in this building. By tomorrow morning I want them all dead. Don't go home until you kill every fly."

The next morning, there wasn't a fly anywhere in the building. For several months, that was his assigned duty. He was the official fly swatter at Best Lock and every day he wore out three fly swatters. Mr. Best was an environmentalist and didn't want to use insecticides in his building, so he paid Reese to eliminate the enemy. "I had a terrific backhand," recalls Reese. "I could kill flies on the forehand and on the backswing."

One day Reese was working in the plant when Mr. Best stopped to talk with him, asking him about his favorite subject in school. Reese told him he liked mechanical drawing and was learning to use a T-square and angles and compasses. Mr. Best beamed with pleasure because he had taught industrial arts in Seattle.

That was a pivotal moment in Reese's life. He was a 17-year-old high school student who had grabbed the interest of a 70-year-old inventor and business owner. Mr. Best went to Reese's boss and said, "Tell Reese to report to my office on Monday and to wear a tie." Mr. Best wanted a young man whom he could mentor and to whom he could pass on his innovations and ideas. He also wanted someone whom he could trust to draw for him and help him develop his plans.

The next Monday, clad in suit and tie, Reese showed up at the president's office. Mr. Best had a table set up behind his desk, outfitted with drafting tools. He started Reese drawing, teaching him how to design sketches for his inventions and products. "I found favor in his eyes and in time I became his assistant," said Reese. "He could have hired any draftsman he wanted—he had a whole engineering department in his plant—but he wanted me in his office where he could mentor me and have me work on projects for him."

When Reese graduated from high school in 1960, he began working full time for Mr. Best. He also enrolled in classes at Indiana University-Purdue University Indianapolis. However, he was working so many hours at Best Lock it became impossible to pursue a formal degree.[75] But under Mr. Best's tutelage, he learned practical engineering skills and how to design metal products through tool and die work. He learned how to use stamping machines and the fastest ways to make anything from metal.

When Mr. Best wanted to build a new plant, he placed Reese in charge of the process. The 19-year-old found himself traveling all over the country, visiting tool and die shops, working with top engineering firms, and figuring out how to build a factory from the ground up. He had to learn about concrete and floor strength and stress factors of buildings containing heavy industrial machinery that vibrated. He learned about horsepower, tool design, machine purchasing, presses, feeders, forklifts, truck docks—everything related to the building of a factory. Then there was the financing of the construction and the banking and the hiring of employees. It was an exhilarating experience, and Reese recalls that he couldn't wait to wake up each morning and get to work. It was incredible that Mr. Best would put a teenager in charge of all that, and others in the company were none too happy. But Reese learned a great deal in a short period and did his work as well as possible.

On October 27, 1963, when Reese turned 21 and could legally sign the papers according to the laws of that day, he was named vice president of Best Lock Company and placed over a new division named Best Products. An industry magazine, Iron Age, ran an article about him, calling him the youngest vice president of any large corporation in America.

All went well for a while, but things began to change when Mr. Best developed diabetes and other health problems. He depended on Reese to care for him. "I pushed him to the doctor's office and went to his house to give him insulin shots," recalls Reese. "He was a stubborn man, and I was the only person who could persuade him to seek medical treatment. We were totally loyal to each other. I was also smart enough to know my days at Best Lock were numbered. I knew as long as Mr. Best was alive, he would protect me within the company; but I knew that his heirs, who were also involved in the company, resented my role."

By then Reese was 24 and ready to start a business of his own. The new factory he designed for Best Products had greater capacity than the company was using, so he began selling that capacity to other industries in the area. His first two customers were RCA Victor and Link-Belt Construction Equipment

Company, and he began overseeing some stamping work for them. When Mr. Best became too ill to work, the pressure from his sons and from others in the company grew stronger. Reese thought more and more about starting his own business in contract metal stamping.

After Frank Best died, Reese left the company and started his own business. Kauffman Products, Inc. was incorporated on June 20, 1967. He managed to leave Best Lock on good terms, and one of the sons, Walt Best, even told him, "One day you are going to be very, very successful and when you are, please tell everyone it was Best Lock that gave you a start."

"Well, it's true," Reese now says. "Best Lock gave me a start and for that I'm very grateful."

CHAPTER 6
Beginnings in Business

WHEN KAUFFMAN PRODUCTS, INC. OPENED ITS DOORS IN 1967, ITS CHANCES OF SUCCESS WERE SLIM. Most business start-ups fail. Reese began his efforts trying to lease portions of the Best Lock factories. When those attempts failed, he left the company with nothing but his experiences and contacts. He had worked hard to make friends with suppliers, clients, bankers, lawyers, and customers. His reputation had spread throughout the industry, and some of the biggest companies in the world, like RCA, began giving him purchase orders. But he was young to be starting his own plant and naïve about the legal and financial machinery needed to support a successful start-up. Walking into Indiana National Bank, Reese approached a man in the teller's window, showed him his purchase orders, and asked, "Are these worth anything?"

The teller called the manager, and the manager called the Vice President of Small Business Development. Reese showed them his purchase orders, told them what he envisioned, and asked their opinion. After studying the paperwork, the bankers encouraged him to proceed. Reese found a lawyer ("He happened to be a Jewish atheist," Reese recalls), incorporated his business and issued stock, maintaining majority stock for himself as the founder, with controlling interest. He sold stock at $500 a share, a figure drawn from the air. He only sought out one investor. All the others came to him. And he didn't let anyone buy more than $5,000 worth of stock (ten shares) because he didn't want anyone else having control. It wasn't a partnership he wanted, just investors (in time he was able to buy them all out and retain full ownership of his company).

Having raised the necessary capital, Reese returned to the bank six weeks after his initial visit to show them the progress he had made and to ask them for a loan to buy a new press. Despite his age—24—the loan was approved in ten minutes. "You've been approved for anything you want," the bankers said.

Reese found an old building in a brickyard in a rundown part of Indianapolis. The building had high ceilings and 4,000 square feet of working space. Reese cleaned it out, bought an air compressor, set up an office area, then traveled to Saginaw, Michigan, to buy his first punch press—a used one—for $10,000. With the money from the bank loan, he ordered a new Federal OBI press. Then he hired one employee, Larry Lee, at $3.75 per hour, which was a decent wage at the time.

"I worked day and night to get my company off the ground," Reese remembers. "At night I shed my dress clothes and worked in the shop, running machinery, driving forklifts, staining my hands with oil and grease, and trying to get quality products out the door. During the day I wore a coat and tie and called on and entertained customers. When I brought in a customer, Larry would fire up the one machine we owned with the one job we had. The minute the customer left we shut the off the machine because we had limited jobs and scarce quantities of steel. We wanted to be able to have the machine running when the next customer showed up to convey the impression of productivity."

For all of his efforts, the prospects appeared bleak. But one very bright spot cast a glow over everything—the glow of candlelight. Reese was falling in love with a woman whose tenacity and sociability matched his own—Linda Watson, whom he first met at Best Lock. They married in 1971 with lots of love but little money. During their first Christmas together, they were too broke to even afford a Christmas tree.

One day, in rare moment of discouragement, Reese said to Linda over lunch, "You know, I don't think we're going to make it."

"You quit talking like that," she said. "It's been predetermined that we're going to make it. Don't ever let me hear you talk like that again."

Reese was determined to build a company that made money day and night, even while he was sleeping. Machines can run all night. They can churn out orders 24 hours a day. They can run three shifts. Reese's attitude became: "If I'm going to build something, why not build something that works around the clock and not just when I'm consciously on the job?"

Little by little, KPI pulled in customers. As orders came in, Reese saw the need for a dependable workforce. One of his biggest problems was getting good employees. "There's a large percentage of people who suffer from an allergy to work," Reese says. "I was hiring common unskilled labor. I used to go down to the day-labor areas or temp services. On some occasions, I picked up hitchhikers and offered them a job."

One day, two uniformed police officers came to the plant to appeal for a donation to the Policeman's Fund. As the officers chatted with him, Reese began to sense something was wrong out on the factory floor. The sounds of the machinery got off rhythm. "To me," he says, "the sound of factory equipment is like an orchestra. You learn its hum and rhythm. As I talked to the officers I sensed a slight change in this hum and rhythm. I excused myself to investigate and discovered I had so many employees who were wanted by the police they had simply abandoned their posts. I found them hiding behind barrels or standing by the rear doors. Some employees I never did see again. They thought the officers had come to the plant looking for them."

Bit by bit, KPI gained a quality workforce to go along with new clients and customers, and the company soon needed to expand. Reese doubled the plant from its original 4,000 square feet to 8,000, then again to 11,000. But there were no adequate truck docks and little room was left for further expansion. The next time KPI ran out of space, it was time for Reese to relocate and build on his own property. He went out to a beautiful industrial park several miles out of town, closer to his home, and built a 22,000 square feet building with spacious offices. He constructed a total of four buildings, all connected; and in a series of expansions KPI increased manufacturing space to 86,000 square feet.

All the while, God was expanding Reese's heart and preparing him for high volume ministry. One of his first efforts at Christian service was teaching an early morning men's Bible study about applying biblical principles to the business world.

It was designed to encourage men before the workday began. The study began at 6:30 a.m. in the Marriott Hotel on the east side of Indianapolis. For 14 years he taught on Friday mornings. Then he added a second Bible study on the west side of town. It required a lot of study. Many times Reese stayed up all night on Thursday preparing his lesson, getting the material finished by dawn. Then he'd take a shower and leave to teach the Bible study. "I put in countless all-nighters," he recalls. "It was 'forced Bible study.' Sometimes that's good for us."

> **"God is always preparing us for future service."**

At the same time Reese was teaching a Sunday school class at his church, which was a verse-by-verse study. He had two Bible studies going on simultaneously for years. "I don't know how beneficial they were for others, but I believe God was using those opportunities to enrich me in His Word and prepare me for the future work He had for me," Reese says. "God is always preparing us for future service. Wherever you are and whatever you're doing, it's simply an ongoing training for future work, whether on Earth or in heaven. In my case, there were three dynamic days that shaped my life—not three days in a row, but three separate days within the span of a few years that consolidated my experiences and set the ultimate direction of my life."

Jesse Irvin Overholtzer

Mr. and Mrs. Overholtzer

Students taking a break during an
early Institute.

An early Children's Ministries Institute.
In 2014 more than 342,000 people were trained worldwide.

First Session of Child Evangelism Institute, January-June, 1945

The first session of Children's Ministries Institute in 1945.

Good News Club (formerly Home Bible Class) in 1961 (page 10).

Good News Club in the 1930s (page 10).

The Treehouse Club

Reese, age 4, decides his sister Nerus needs to be saved (page 40).

Reese, age 14.

Kauffman family when Reese was 17.

Reese with one of his first 250-ton presses.
Inset photo: Reese at Kauffman Products, Inc. in the 1960s. The sign still hangs in his office today.

"Sometimes we feel like our son Bucky grew up on an airplane."

Reese and Linda with their children Michelle, Rock and Bucky.

Reese and his mother, Neva (page 40).

Reese in Cyprus to encourage missionaries.

Reese and close friend and prayer partner, Larry Green (page 194).

Reese and dear friend, Buzz Baker, at the White House.

Reese and Buzz enjoying the outdoors.

A snowy day at CEF International Headquarters.

Reese with Sam Doherty in Luzern, Switzerland.

Reese and Bucky celebrate Russ Kauffman's 96th birthday.

Typical impromptu conversation at a CEF conference.

Reese at Red Square in Moscow in 1990.

Reese with national missionaries in West and Central Africa region.

CEF of Nigeria National Office in Kaduna.

Reese and Linda having fun with the CEF family.

Reese loves being on the water.

Reese congratulating Dottie Whitney on 50 years of service with CEF.

Reese teaching children.

Reese with Saint in Swaziland.

Reese speaking at the 2013 European Conference while Gerd-Walter Buskies, Regional Director for CEF Europe, translates.

Good News Club at a school in Madagascar.

Good News Across America in Indianapolis, Indiana.

Dedication of CEF facility in Japan.

Children's Ministries Institute in Sri Lanka.

Good News Club at a school in Rwanda.

5-Day Club
in the 1960s.

5-Day Club
today.

All around
the world,
children
hear the
Gospel in
Good New
Club.

Good News Club in India.

5-Day Club
in Mexico.

Mike Petkof
teaching in a
Gypsy camp
in Greece.

Terenik Barjamian (inset), National Director of CEF of Armenia, sharing the Gospel at a Good News Club outside Yerevan.

Children in the Philippines reading *Every Day with God*, a daily devotional.

Teaching children about Jesus in Latvia.

Teens in India.

Aerial view of CEF International Headquarters.

Reese at the International Plaza at CEF International Headquarters.

CHAPTER 7

Three Unforgettable Days

T HE BIBLE FREQUENTLY POINTS TO THE IMPORTANCE OF "THREE DAYS." On the third day, God created the land and seas with the plants and seeds (Genesis 1:13). On the third day, Abraham and Isaac arrived at Mount Moriah, where Abraham, by faith, demonstrated his willingness to offer his son as a burnt offering for sin, prefiguring the work Christ would do (Genesis 22:4). On the third day, God appeared to the children of Israel in the desert (Exodus 19:11-16). The Israelites later prepared for three days to cross the River Jordan and enter the Promised Land (Joshua 1:11). Hosea 6:2 says, "After two days he will revive us; on the third day he will raise us up, that we may live before him." Jesus told His disciples, "Just as Jonah was three days and three nights in the belly of the great fish, so will the Son of Man be three days and three nights in the heart of the earth" (Matthew 12:40). He told the Jewish leaders, "Destroy this temple, and in three days I will raise it up" (John 2:19). And the Bible tells us: "Christ died for our sins in accordance with the Scriptures... he was buried... he was raised on the third day" (1 Corinthians 15:3-4).

The biblical pattern of three days also provides the framework for Reese Kauffman's testimony. They focus on the triple themes of Knowledge, Relationship, and Service—knowing God intimately, talking with Him faithfully, and serving Him passionately.

Day One

The First Day occurred in 1972, five years into Reese's business career. At 29, he was still following his mother's daily rule: "Brush your teeth and read your Bible." She had so drilled that habit into his daily routine that even as a hardworking business owner he always made sure he read a chapter of Scripture before falling asleep at night.

One night his reading took him to Psalm 139. As he read that passage, two verses flew off the page and struck him with a jolt: "How precious to me are your thoughts, O God! How vast is the sum of them! If I would count them, they are more than the sand" (Psalm 139:17-18a).

Reese recalls, "Somehow I had never before realized God was thinking of me in such comprehensive and constant terms. I was a Christian businessman, but at that time I was not yet living aggressively for the Lord. My heart was all business with little time left over for Him. I knew He ordered the paths of the stars and controlled the tides of the sea, but I didn't realize He was concerned about my afternoon appointment with a customer. If His thoughts of me were more than the sands on the shore, He was surely thinking about what was taking up most of my time—my business. I'd not really considered the fact that God was thinking about my business even more than I was. I would work for months to get a 20-minute appointment with an executive of GE, but I never thought that God might have a hand in orchestrating those appointments. If His thoughts to me were so vast, I realized, should I not be seeking to intimately know the God who so intimately knows me?"

From that night Reese's life became a pursuit of God's presence, His will, and His blessings in every area. He deeply desired to know the Lord better each day and let Him have controlling interest over all the affairs of life, including his business affairs.

"My background had been steeped in Christianity," says Reese. "I'd grown up in a parsonage listening to my dad's sermons and hearing my mom read the Bible every morning. I had asked Christ to be my Savior when I was eight years old. I was a faithful church attendee and had always practiced the habit of tithing. But my nocturnal encounter with Psalm 139 was as dramatic as the one Nicodemus had experienced with Christ in John 3, and it represented a new phase in my spiritual zeal.

> "He is important, supreme, and sovereign, and He wants us to recognize Him as such over even the smallest issues of life."

"My view of God began to change from that moment. Everything we do in life depends on our view of God. He is important, supreme, and sovereign, and He wants us to recognize Him as such over even the smallest issues of life. If He is omnipresent, He sees everything we do. It's insane to try to do everything on our own if we really believe God oversees our lives, down to the last details. It's especially foolish to cut corners, shortchange taxes, overcharge customers, or waste our resources.

"As I pondered this, I saw another verse in the Bible. A little sentence in 3 John says, 'Beloved, I pray that you may prosper in all things and be in health, just as your soul prospers' (3 John 1:2).[76] The apostle John offered that prayer for his friend Gaius, and I found it impacting. I understood from that verse that I should ask God to prosper me physically and financially to the same extent as my soul was prospering—no more, no less. That verse took hold of me, and I began praying, 'Lord, I don't want my business to prosper more than I am prospering in my walk with You. Don't let my business grow beyond my own spiritual growth.' That became my prayer."

Reese shared this insight with his pastor, Dwaine Felber. To Reese's chagrin his prayer soon became public. It happened at a groundbreaking for KPI's first new plant on the recently acquired property. The crowd gathered on an outdoor site around shovels, easels, pictures, and drawings of the new plant. The employees were there, along with customers, suppliers, and dignitaries. Reese had asked his pastor to say a few words. As the pastor finished speaking, he commented, "I don't know if you know this about Reese, but he has asked the Lord that his business not prosper beyond his relationship with God. So if you see this business failing, it may be that he is failing spiritually!"

That day Reese determined by God's grace he would not fail spiritually. His appetite for Scripture became so great that he started showing up for every service at church with his Bible and notebook in hand, waiting impatiently through the singing and announcements, ready to click his pen and take notes during the teaching of God's Word. "If God's thoughts toward me were as vast as the sand on the seashores," says Reese, "I wanted my thoughts to be consistently focused on Him and on His Word."

Day Two

The Second Day came in 1974, when Reese attended a Sunday evening service in which evangelist Fred Brown was preaching on the subject of prayer. "Tomorrow when you drive to work," said the preacher, "take your right hand and turn the knob to the left and spend time talking with God." Reese realized Brown was telling them to turn off their radios so they could spend time in prayer.

The next morning, Reese slid behind the wheel of his black Pontiac Grand Prix and started the ignition. Radio station WIBC came on, the station he listened to each day during his 12-minute commute. Remembering what the preacher had said the previous night, Reese reached over and turned the radio knob to the off position. He spent his drive time that morning talking with the Lord, and by afternoon he felt the day had been different. Walking to his car to return home, he decided to continue the experiment. "After all," he observes, "how a man enters his house at night sets the tone for his family. If we walk through the door exhausted and exasperated and carrying the burdens of the day, we'll transfer that to our families. But it's different if we drive home saying, 'Now the most important part of my day is coming home, being with my wife and children. I'll just pray about that.'"

> **Reese learned to make his commute home a holy time in the Lord's presence.**

In this way, Reese learned to make his commute home a holy time in the Lord's presence. He planned his drive-time prayer each evening so as he walked up the sidewalk and reached to touch the doorknob, he was just finishing his prayer, saying, "In Jesus' name. Amen."

Day Two signaled the beginning of a life of growing dependence on prayer. It wasn't just a matter of praying in the car on the way to work; it was the growing awareness that wherever he was—in the car, at home, at work, on the water or in the air—he could enjoy the conscious presence of God.

"I thought I knew how to pray. I prayed before meals, at bedtime, at church. But on that day after hearing Fred Brown's sermon, it was different; it was more of a relationship with God, of bringing Him into the day I was about to start. And on the way home, it was a matter of talking with the Lord about the things that had happened. It was a new experience to bring God so tangibly into my day, making Him part of my business, talking with Him as though He were sitting in the front seat with me—which He was."

Reese's prayer time is now the most important part of his day. As we'll discuss later, he admits to being almost legalistic in his prayer commitment. "I can't put my head on the pillow unless I've completed my daily prayer time, praying for those people and items for which I've committed to pray," he says. "I've not missed a day in completing my prayer list in over 30 years. At night I often go on a prayer walk. After the day's work is over, I'll find a trail and walk and pray and talk with the Lord as if chatting with a close companion—which He is."

Reese strives to practice the presence of the Lord wherever he goes, in travels far and wide. His prayer list is always with him. "I can pray wherever I am," he says, "because I can never get away from the Lord's omnipresent nearness. Our ministry is filled with praying men, women, and children. It's the secret of our work at CEF. I can tell you with confidence that Child Evangelism Fellowship is nothing more than a string of answered prayer."

PAINKILLER?

Kimber Kauffman recalls a time when Reese was in the hospital recovering from kidney stones. He was in considerable pain and it was time for an injection of painkiller. But when the doctor arrived with the shot, Reese begged off. "Doctor, would you mind coming back in about ten minutes?"

The doctor agreed, but Kimber was puzzled. "Reese, you're in tremendous pain. Why didn't you let the doctor give you the shot now?"

Reese answered, "The shot will put me to sleep, and I don't want to fall asleep until I finish my prayer list."

Day Three

The Third Day came a year later, in 1975, as Reese sat in church listening to a missionary from Latin America. This man—Reese can't even recall his name—was talking about his ministry while Reese fidgeted and waited for him to open the Scriptures. "I had an insatiable desire for Bible study," Reese recalls, "and I expected biblical content to sermons. I had my notebook and pen in hand. But all this man was talking about was his ministry. I realized he really didn't even want to be there in that worship service; he wanted to be on the mission field. He needed financial support. He was passionate about the work God had given him, and he couldn't wait to get back to doing it."

The Holy Spirit whispered: "That man has something you don't—a personal ministry he believes in." It suddenly dawned on Reese that there was more to serving Christ than Bible study, as rich and valuable as that is. There is Christian service, and Bible study that doesn't result in service is sheer gluttony. Reese felt something was still missing in his life. He needed an outlet to serve the Lord with all his heart.

At the end of the service the pastor invited people to come forward if they wanted to make a significant spiritual decision in their life. Reese stepped forward. "What decision have you reached?" asked the pastor.

"I don't know that I've reached a decision," Reese said. "I've just realized I want to do something for God."

The pastor directed him to the adjacent prayer room where a man named Roy Daniels asked, "What decision have you reached?"

"I don't know that I've reached a decision," Reese said. "I've just realized I want to do something for God."

Roy's eyes brightened and he asked, "Have you ever heard of CEF?"

"Doesn't that have something to do with children?"

"Yes. It's Child Evangelism Fellowship."

At that point, Reese lost some interest. He'd never thought of himself as a children's missionary. Nevertheless, he agreed to have lunch with Dave Birch, the CEF director for Indianapolis. Over lunch, Dave invited him to attend the next local CEF committee meeting to be held at the home of a doctor who was involved in the work. Reese went hesitantly, wondering if he really wanted to be drawn into a ministry like this. But as he sat listening to the CEF missionaries describe their work; he was astounded at the reports of the number of children coming to the Lord.

"If these people are telling the truth," Reese said to himself, "the little group in this room is leading more souls to Christ than all the churches in Indianapolis." Reese knew the church scene in his city. He knew that many churches were seeing an individual converted now and again, but the CEF missionaries in that room were describing an avalanche of souls. Reese was astounded to learn that this is not unusual. The majority of people who come to Christ do so by their 15th birthday. As a high volume manufacturer, that appealed to Reese. That evening he was invited to join the local CEF committee.

At the second committee meeting, Dave Birch's wife Fran shared a testimony. She said, "Recently while Dave was on a trip to the CEF Headquarters in Warrenton, my parents came to stay with me. Dave wanted to leave me some money, but there weren't enough funds in the CEF bank account to issue his paycheck. I looked in the pantry and had enough staples to get by, but we didn't have any meat. I wasn't sure how to feed my parents, so I went to Dave's study to pray. Looking out the window, I saw my parents drive up. They were early, and I almost panicked. I went out and hugged my mom while my dad was getting something out of the trunk. 'Honey,' he said, 'we brought you this cooler of meat. I'm afraid this roast on top has started to thaw. Do you think you could use it tonight for supper?'"

Fran told that story as a testimony to answered prayer, which it was. But something about it left Reese troubled because the testimony itself was evidence the work was suffering from poor financial underpinning.

After Fran's testimony, the committee conducted its business and the members were asked if they had contacted potential ministry partners or written thank-you notes to contributors. Reese filed this away in his thinking, and he left the meeting with a growing burden for Child Evangelism Fellowship in Indianapolis.

His first chance to actually see the ministry in action occurred at the Indiana State Fair. He was assigned the job of passing out tracts and inviting people to the CEF booth. That evening he saw three boys come to faith in Christ. As time went by, he began noticing how many Christians said they were converted at the age of five, or six, or seven. He also learned how many Christian leaders had been saved in childhood, and he felt a rising passion for child evangelism.

After all, Reese was a businessman whose expertise was high volume manufacturing—loud, rhythmic machines; high production; raw material going in and finished goods coming out. He began realizing that child evangelism is the "high production" aspect of Christianity. In God's Kingdom, the high volume and the high impact are with children. That's where the action is— the fruitfulness, the real results. The similarities between CEF and KPI struck him forcibly.

Still, he hesitated to get involved. He didn't feel gifted as a children's missionary, but he did wonder if there was a role he could fill in encouraging and helping those who were gifted as children's missionaries. He grew enthusiastic about the Indianapolis CEF chapter and found himself speaking at CEF banquets and giving counsel to the missionaries. Before long, he was named chairman of the local committee.

"I remember the first meeting I chaired," Reese says. "We met in the conference room of my plant. In studying the financial reports, I grew alarmed at the need. When I inquired of our treasurer, I learned that local churches were giving only small amounts to the work, and only two of the committee members were regular contributors."

"Don't tell me who they are," Reese told the treasurer. "I don't want to know. We have a committee of a dozen people, and ten of them are not supporting the work." He knew he and Linda were sending a monthly check; so of the remaining eleven committee members, only one was a financial supporter.

Reese called the meeting to order—the first CEF meeting he had ever chaired—gave the devotions, then told them he'd learned something. "We have serious financial issues," he said, "and only two people in this room are giving regularly. You asked me to chair this group, but I don't want to go forward if you're not behind this ministry. If your heart is with CEF and what we're doing here, then let's get behind it. The committee has to lead."

The committee did lead, and the needed funds fell into place. So did Reese's commitment to doing all he could to advance the cause of child evangelism and the ministry of Child Evangelism Fellowship.

CHAPTER 8

Industrial Grade Lessons

THOUGH REESE WAS INCREASINGLY BEING DRAWN INTO THE MINISTRY OF CHILD EVANGELISM FELLOWSHIP, HIS PRIMARY CONCERN WAS STILL HIS BUSINESS. He was building an industrial complex in Indianapolis that was touching the world with innovative products—car horns, fan blades, manifolds, and seatbelts for millions of automobiles; range tops for stoves; television frames and TV transformer end shields; and after-bodies and tail sections for practice bombs for all branches of the U.S. military. His commercial enterprise still occupied the lion's share of his time, and he thought of himself as a manufacturer who donated portions of his time, energy, money, and expertise to the Lord for His work. He didn't yet realize his experiences in high volume manufacturing were preparing him to lead a high volume ministry. Looking back, Kauffman Products, Inc. was God's schoolhouse to prepare Reese for leading a global evangelistic mission. While many Christian leaders wisely seek their training in Bible schools, seminaries, and on-field experiences, another category of leadership can arise from the world of business, manufacturing, trade, and commerce. After all, every business can be a ministry; and every ministry needs to operate with the financial integrity of a good business.

While it's impossible to recount all Reese's experiences along the way, there are a few unforgettable stories and indelible lessons he shares with friends. These are moments that prepared him for his future responsibilities at Child Evangelism Fellowship.

OSHA

One of KPI's most memorable challenges involved OSHA—The Occupational Safety and Health Administration. This agency came into being after President Richard Nixon signed the Occupational Safety and Health Act in 1970 to assure safe working conditions in private and public enterprises. OSHA came onto the scene shortly after Reese went into business, and in the early days it was frightening to have an inspector show up. No one argues its importance, but it was nearly impossible to understand all their regulations or meet all their standards. Keeping employees safe is everyone's business, something KPI undertook with utmost seriousness. Still, Reese found it hard to feel positive about an OSHA visit, because this was a governmental agency that could shut down a factory at any time.

One day in the early 1980s, Reese was in his plant office when an OSHA inspector entered the lobby. That sent a chill up Reese's spine, but he soon realized things were beyond his worst fears. "Mr. Kauffman," said the inspector, "I'm not here for a routine inspection. One of your workers turned in a disgruntled employee report claiming there are unsafe practices at your plant."

The man detailed the accusations, and Reese felt as if one of his children had reported him to social services. As he accompanied the man on an inspection of the factory, a young fellow approached them and asked, "Are you OSHA? I want to talk to you. I'm the one who turned in the report."

That was information neither the OSHA inspector nor the factory owner was supposed to know, but the young man continued, "I don't care who knows. Let me show you the violations."

Both Reese and the inspector were baffled, but Reese said, "Go ahead and show him the plant. I'll not go with you." Returning to his office, Reese engaged in earnest prayer. "Lord," he said, "I'm not David and those people are not the Philistines, but it surely feels like it. I have a disgruntled employee right now probing my plant with an OSHA inspector and I need your help. They could close down my company."

Meanwhile the disgruntled employee showed the OSHA inspector every violation he could find from one end of the plant to the other. Almost two hours later, the inspector walked into the offices. "Mr. Kauffman," he said, "I've been through your plant and I think you're a man who runs a safe operation and tries to protect your people. This young man is obviously upset and angry. I am writing you up as a safe company that cares about its people and runs a safe operation."

Reese silently praised the Lord.

About a week later, a second OSHA inspector showed up in the lobby. With a sinking feeling, Reese asked him, "Are you aware we had an inspection just a week ago?"

"Yes," said the man. "That's why I'm here. You were given a perfect record. That's never been done before in Indiana. I'm the head of OSHA for this state. A perfect record has never been granted out of my office. I wanted to come and inspect the factory with a perfect record." This man, too, left with a commendation for KPI.

And the disgruntled employee? He wasn't fired or disciplined, but the passing of time proved he had other problems and he eventually left on his own. "The whole incident taught me a good lesson," Reese recalls. "Integrity speaks for itself and bears its own testimony. And in moments of pressure, prayer can turn trials into trophies."

General Motors

Sometime later, an even worse threat knocked on Reese's door—General Motors. In its heyday, GM had several brands—Chevrolet, Oldsmobile, Buick, Cadillac, Pontiac —all of them needing car horns. KPI acquired a contract to make all the horns for all the vehicles. Every GM product produced in America would carry a horn built in the Kauffman plant in Indianapolis. Every car has at least one horn, and some have two. KPI was in production 24 hours a day, 7 days a week. They stockpiled hundreds of thousands of car horns in a 20,000-square-foot warehouse with ceilings 24 feet high.

On corporate Christmas Eve—the last day of work before the holidays—while the plant workers were celebrating together, Reese got a message that all the horns were defective and could not be used—not one of them. He went into his plant and as far as he could see there was nothing but car horns. The impact of that message hitting him during the Christmas season was terrible. All those beautiful parts were nothing but worthless scrap. The whole investment was a staggering liability.

Reese immediately drove up to Detroit, arriving at the GM plant during a corporate Christmas party there. It was surreal—

amid the celebrations and cheer of that moment, to hear the news in person. The horns were worthless. Returning home, he told his workers the products were flawed, the inventory was worthless, their jobs were in jeopardy, and the company was in crisis.

Reese cried out to God for mercy. For two weeks, everyone at KPI lived under a cloud. Reese prayed earnestly and sought to trust the Lord with the burden. His life's work was collapsing—at least his commercial life.

After the first of the year, the director of purchasing for General Motors came down and listened as Reese made the case for the accuracy of KPI's work. "What did it cost you to produce those horns?" the man asked. "I want you to calculate all your costs, put it into a bill, and send it to me. Our investigations show we sent you the wrong die. It wasn't your fault; it was ours. We sent you a tool from the morgue. All those weeks you put into the design and production of those horns, charge it to us. We'll bear the responsibility and reimburse you for all your expenses."

Looking back on the incident, Reese says, "This was an unbelievable act of integrity for General Motors. When the check came from GM, the payment allowed me to buy an adjacent piece of land to expand our plant. What appeared to be a disaster turned out to be a great blessing. Those who practice integrity and concern and fairness find the blessings of God. And those who pray over their problems and commit them to the Lord in simple trust and obedience find that He really does work all things for good. God delivered our company, in answer to our prayers."

The Canoe

In 1 Samuel 7, the prophet Samuel, having led Israel in victory over the Philistines, erected a stone monument called Ebenezer—"Stone of Help." Every tenured Christian knows what it's like to look back over life and see mile markers that commemorate significant lessons learned or victories won. For Reese Kauffman, one of those Ebenezers is shaped like a canoe.

It happened at the end of a hard week. As Reese drove home on a Friday afternoon, he was battling deep discouragement. He had lost four major accounts that week—customers he'd worked hard to develop. Losing just one of them would have been a blow, but to lose all four in one week was enough to put a dent in even the most galvanized optimist. Reese could foresee his business crashing down around him.

Seeing his face as he walked into the house, Linda said, "Why don't you take the canoe out on the river and relax a little bit?" The Kauffmans lived alongside White River, the only river flowing through Indianapolis. Reese launched the canoe and started paddling upstream toward the bridge.

He recalls, "As I paddled I talked to myself, a technique I've practiced over the years, asking myself questions, working through my emotions verbally. Is God sovereign over my affairs? Yes. He's absolutely sovereign. Does He love me? Yes, with a love beyond any human love that could be comprehended. Would God hurt me? No. He would never hurt me. He's my Heavenly Father who works everything for my good. If those things are true, what am I worried about? I don't know. The cloud lifted. My countenance changed and my joy returned. As I turned the canoe around and returned to the house, I was a different man, prompting Linda to ask what happened to me."

> **"I also realized afresh that it grieves the Lord when we don't trust Him."**

Looking back, Reese says it was obvious the Lord was cleaning house and removing some smaller accounts that probably weren't very profitable anyway. "He cleared them out of my agenda to make room for larger and better accounts that were coming. I also realized afresh that it grieves the Lord when we don't trust Him. He has never once failed us. I can't tell you how many times both in business and in ministry I've had to metaphorically get back into that canoe and remind myself that whenever I am fretting, it's because I'm not thinking biblically or seeing clearly."

Jenn-Air

In 1947, Louis J. Jenn founded an Indianapolis-based company called Jenn-Air, which specialized in kitchen appliances. For many years, KPI made their stovetops. These were cosmetic stainless steel products that had to be perfect, without a trace of a dent, ding, or scratch. Jenn-Air was one of Kauffman's early customers, and their business amounted to millions of dollars for the company.

One day, Reese got a call from the Director of Purchasing, who wanted to come over and see him. Reese was concerned, because his factory was full of employees dependent on the Jenn-Air account. "If they come with tubes and files tucked under their arms," he told his coworkers, "they're coming with new work. If they come empty-handed they're going to close their account with us."

Reese made a conscious decision not to worry, instead making it a matter of prayer and leaving it totally in God's hands. When the men arrived a few days later, they carried nothing in their arms. Sitting in Reese's office, one of the men said, "Reese, you know the work we gave you is not permanent. We're having some issues with things on our end, some problems with the union. We're going to have to end our agreements with you."

As they left, Reese's mind went into overdrive. His plant had two more weeks of work with Jenn-Air, and then the presses would start shutting down one by one. Yet Reese wasn't gripped by fear nor was his stomach tied in knots. Somehow, God gave him faith to remain calm enough to see what would happen.

Two weeks passed, and the inventory of stainless steel was running low as the presses fabricated the last of the Jenn-Air products. Then the phone rang. "Reese, you know the work we were going to take away? Well, I've just come out of a meeting, and I want to tell you that we're not going to take it away after all. We're going to increase it." And they did, resulting in more jobs, more products, and more prosperity for KPI and its employees.

Years later, Reese recalled the lesson he learned from that experience. "It's easy to live in fear when you're in business," he said. "Losing a customer or a client can be devastating, not only to the business owners but to the employees and their families. But as I learned to trust the Lord to work out those things, I found a calmness that was almost unexplainable. Throughout the strain of the Jenn-Air crisis, I had peace. We became a steady supplier for Jenn-Air for the next 15 years. I remember that valley very well; but I didn't suffer as I sometimes do, because the Lord enabled me to trust Him to work it out."

The Aggravator

Those who know Reese appreciate his graciousness, professionalism, and warm smile. But there was one man who tried his best to get under Reese's skin and almost succeeded. "One day the Director of Purchasing for Jenn-Air retired," Reese recalls, "and instead of promoting someone from within the company they hired a new person from the outside, a man named Phil. I was warned in advance that I wouldn't like Phil, and that proved accurate. Phil was argumentative, adversarial, and crude. For two years he did everything he could to upset me."

One day, learning Reese was speaking at a college, this man called and chewed him out just before his lecture. The purpose seemed to be an attempt to spoil his frame of mind before his speaking engagement. On another occasion, Phil invited him to lunch with a handful of other executives. Over the meal he spouted nonstop criticism of KPI and its leadership. Then Phil bolted from the table, leaving Reese to pay the check. "I have an important meeting at two o'clock," Phil said.

Reese fumed over the snubs and tried to exercise the kind of self-control that befits a Christian, but it was tough. Vexing people have a way of getting to us, and it's hard not to retaliate. If nothing else, our minds get preoccupied with how we might retaliate should we decide to. Clearly, there are times when we need to defend ourselves, stand up to bullies, and express a reasoned point of view. But other times, it's best to wait to see how God will handle the matter. In this case, the Lord resolved things quickly. The very next morning Reese received a call from a friend at Jenn-Air named Brent Hopping, who had never before called him at home.

"I thought you'd want to know," Brent said, "Phil was fired yesterday during a two o'clock meeting over here. He actually left lunch with you to come back to Jenn-Air to get fired."

Apparently Phil had trouble getting along with a lot of people, not just Reese.

In speaking to business leaders and people involved in ministry organizations, Reese often tells this story to underline the importance of understanding organizational authority structures. The Bible clearly teaches that God has ordained all authority. This world is held together by authority structure. Everything ordained by God exhibits a system of authority and responsibility—home, marriage, children, church, government, and business. God uses the existence of authority structures to accomplish His purposes, even when those authorities are not perfect.

One authority that comes into the lives of business leaders is their customer base. The customer has the right to give or take away business. "In a sense," Reese explains, "I found myself under Phil's authority, for he was my customer. Though he was difficult, I had to respect that authority and try to meet his expectations. I don't know why God placed him in my life for two years. He plagued me week after week, but I still looked to him as an authority and tried to show respect. Sometime later, I called my friend Brent and asked him why he had given me the news of the firing, which was inside information for Jenn-Air."

"Everyone knew he hated your guts," Brent said.

"Why?"

"I don't know. I think he was just jealous."

We never know when we'll be working with a rotten boss, a bad teacher, a difficult coworker, or a frustrating leader in some area of our life. Yes, we can stand up for our rights. We can explain and defend and keep others from abusing us. But we must still exercise an underlying respect for authority. "You've got to remember the hand of God is working through all these things," says Reese.

ANOTHER CALL

I recently had another call from Brent Hopping. "Do you remember," he said, "when we lived in Indianapolis, and you and I used to drive to Cincinnati on factory visits? I dreaded those trips, because I usually had a hangover from the previous night and I knew you'd start talking to me about the Lord."

This was true. I always looked for opportunities to witness to my associates. At meals, I'd always ask, "Would you mind if I thanked the Lord for my food?"

With Brent, some of those seeds planted by me and by others finally sprouted, and he called to tell me he had trusted the Lord Jesus Christ as Savior. I marveled at the way the Lord used few words and actions to bring a hard-hearted and hard-drinking businessman to Himself. Another man who came to the Lord was Jack Lou, a Chinese gentleman who came to Indianapolis to design the airport. He later designed my plant. He received Christ as his Savior while sitting in my office. The Bible is absolutely right when it assures us our labor in the Lord is not in vain.

–Reese Kauffman

The importance of understanding and working within authority structures is a crucial biblical skill, one that can make the difference between failure and success. One day, a man came to Reese seeking counsel. The man was very professional and had excellent communication skills. He was well-dressed and made a good appearance. But there were several companies in Indianapolis in his line of work, and he had worked for just about all of them. When Reese asked him about his last job, he said, "My boss was an unprofessional man, a jerk."

"What about the job before that?"

"Oh, you wouldn't believe my boss there."

"What about the job before that?"

"Oh, they have management issues...."

Listening, Reese thought to himself, Maybe all he says about his bosses is true, but his lack of respect for the authority structures over him has sullied his reputation from one end of Indianapolis to the other.

The Bible tells us we should respect our earthly employers when they are right, but also when they are unreasonable and unfair (1 Peter 2:13-25). Of course, we mustn't obey them or follow their advice when they tell us to do something wrong (Acts 5:29), but our reputations and livelihoods depend on a healthy respect for authority.

"We develop these attitudes at an early age," says Reese. "That's one of the reasons God places children in homes with parents over them, to teach them the importance of working within authority systems. If you don't respect authority, you are not respecting God. If you have a correct view of authority and show respect for it, you'll be a good child, a good employee, a good student, a good worker, a good citizen. It foreshadows a successful life."

"Can I Start Monday?"

To Reese Kauffman, a person's character and reputation must be built on honesty, and as the head of a sprawling manufacturing business, he was forever trying to teach employees the importance of integrity.

"One day I walked through my plant, which had developed into a large operation with many employees. Glancing through the windows into the lobby, I noticed a young man from my church. Because I knew the young man's father very well, I went to greet the fellow, who, as it turns out, was looking for a job. Normally I would have sent him to the personnel department, but I'd just left the bomb line where the bombs were being assembled and had learned we were one worker short. Nine guys worked on that line and they were the hardest workers in the building."

"I might know of an opening," Reese told the young man, "but this is the hardest part of the building and the people who work there are the hardest workers we have."

"That's fine. I'll do anything."

"Well, come and watch them for a few minutes and make sure," Reese told him, escorting the young man to a place where he could safely watch the assembly line. It was an energetic crew, working in rhythm, even singing in time.

"You can start tomorrow morning at 8:00," Reese said.

"Well," said the young man, hesitating, "I have some things to do tomorrow. Is it possible to start on Monday?"

That was an ominous sign, especially since the young man had been out of work for nine weeks and had a wife and family to support. But after a pause Reese said, "Okay. You can start Monday."

Monday morning he showed up, went through the paperwork, got his equipment, and joined the crew. He lasted an hour and a half, then disappeared. He didn't clock out. Didn't say goodbye. Didn't explain. He just left the building. The worst part is during his scant 90 minutes on the job, he had told everyone, "I'm a personal friend of Reese Kauffman. I'm a member of Reese's church, and I'm a Christian."

He left behind a negative testimony.

"Everyone knows us by how we work," says Reese. "It's not just what we say or the words we speak. This young fellow cheapened the cause of Christ, the reputation of our church, and my own name because he didn't approach his work as something to be done as unto the Lord.

"Colossians 3:23-24 is a key text in how we should go about our daily work: Whatever you do, work heartily, as for the Lord and not for men, knowing that from the Lord you will receive the inheritance as your reward. You are serving the Lord Christ.

"Christians should be the best at whatever they do," says Reese. "If you're cleaning restrooms the way I did starting out, they should be the cleanest restrooms possible because you're cleaning them for the glory of God. Our labor is a form of worship. If we take a lot of shortcuts and a lot of time off, we're not working wholeheartedly for the Lord. It erodes our reputation and discounts our testimony. Our job is a higher calling than we realize.

> **"Our labor is a form of worship. If we take a lot of shortcuts and a lot of time off, we're not working wholeheartedly for the Lord."**

"If a company hires a Christian, they should be hiring the best there is. People should want to hire Christians. Look at the passages in Proverbs about laziness. Some people will use any excuse to minimize their work ethic, but Christians need to be faithful at whatever God gives them to do. I tell my children to always remember they aren't working for a company; they are working for God. This is a basic life-truth we need to instill in our employees and workers, and in our children and grandchildren."

The Sign

"When we built our new plant in 1977," Reese recalls, "it had a nice office building in front that was attached to the plant, and I decided to erect a sign in the lobby that said: 'This Business is Dedicated to Bring Honor and Glory to Jesus Christ.'"

Reese had been inspired by the example of Stanley Tam, the founder of U.S. Plastic Corporation and a stellar businessman, who had sought means to appropriately share the Gospel with customers, clients, suppliers, and employees. The sign Reese envisioned for the KPI offices was designed with white porcelain letters. It would be the first thing people saw when entering the lobby. But as Reese watched the sign company putting up the letters, he had second thoughts. If KPI had customers who became disgruntled or there was a misunderstanding with a vendor, it might damage the very cause Reese wanted to promote. "I've got my Savior's name on the wall," he told himself. "If I put the sign up I've got to live by it."

> **"I've got my Savior's name on the wall," he told himself. "If I put the sign up I've got to live by it."**

As Reese pondered those things, the owner of the sign company approached him. "Reese," said the man, "I know you're busy today, but if you have time would you tell me what that sign means?"

The sign wasn't even up yet, but it had already opened an opportunity to witness. "Over the years, many people asked about the words on that sign and their meaning," Reese says. "It gave many opportunities to share my faith. I've led people to the Lord in my office because that sign helped arouse their interest. In today's culture we might worry that such signage isn't politically correct, but in the culture of those days my greatest fear was that we might not live up to its message. It kept us on our toes and on our knees. It reflected the deepest desire of my heart as a businessman."

There are hundreds of other stories tucked away in the business files of Reese Kauffman's brain—too many to tell here. But from these experiences came the lessons that prepared Reese to assume the leadership of the world's largest mission to children. Unbeknownst to him at the time, the Lord was about to take him from high volume manufacturing to high volume ministry—with Child Evangelism Fellowship.

CHAPTER 9

From High Volume Manufacturing to High Volume Ministry

A S A BUSINESSMAN AND AS CHAIRMAN OF THE LOCAL CEF COMMITTEE IN INDIANAPOLIS, REESE WAS INVITED TO THE INTERNATIONAL HEADQUARTERS OF CHILD EVANGELISM FELLOWSHIP IN WARRENTON, MISSOURI, TO GIVE HIS TESTIMONY TO THE INTERNATIONAL BOARD OF TRUSTEES FOR CONSIDERATION AS A PROSPECTIVE BOARD MEMBER.

He and Linda drove to Warrenton in their new Cadillac. Reese remembers the trip well, because on the way back Linda spilled an entire cup of coffee on its western saddle interior. When they walked into the Board meeting they quickly realized they were walking into a room filled with confusion. The meeting was tense, and as Reese listened he discerned that one of the men, Gordon Wood, had made some difficult and unpopular financial decisions. Recognizing the dangerous state of the financial books, Wood had moved to protect the organization's financial integrity.

Reese listened all day long with his businessman's hat on, and when the time came for his testimony, he spoke plainly, telling them, "I don't know who this man Gordon Wood is, but someone should thank him because it sounds like he has saved this organization."

That was not, generally speaking, the view of the Board, and when Reese proceeded to give his testimony, it's questionable whether anyone heard it. The members were still reeling from his opening observation. Afterward, Dave Birch, the man who had nominated Reese for the position, leaned over his shoulder and whispered, "You've just insured yourself not being put on the Board."

That was fine with Reese; it wasn't necessarily a position anyone would have wanted at that moment. CEF was going through a time that left the ministry fractured and struggling. Yet somehow Reese was put on the Board; and in 1979, he became vice chairman. In 1981, at age 39, he was appointed chairman.

Meanwhile back in Indianapolis, KPI moved into its first new plant. Reese watched over his financial and manufacturing enterprises, yet more of his time was preoccupied with CEF. "I loved business," Reese recalls, "but my heart was moving into the Lord's work in a way that was almost beyond my control. I recall being involved in the Chamber of Commerce for our community, and I took up sign ordinances and streetlights and paving roads. But I kept asking myself why I was devoting my time to sign ordinances when I could be helping CEF figure out more ways to reach children for Christ."

Reese visited Poland to teach the Bible at the invitation of Sam Doherty, the head of CEF work in Europe. These were Iron Curtain days, and for two weeks Reese taught the Bible in a Communist land. His lodgings were in an old Lutheran monastery and he walked three miles each day to the location of the CEF Institute classes where 30 or 40 Polish young people were training for children's ministry. Each day he kept a wary eye open for the secret police, but there was no interference in the work.

During these long walks with Sam Doherty, Reese learned of fierce debates among CEF missionaries over various theological and organizational issues. He later credited those hours with Doherty for giving him the insights needed to circumvent divisions and avert splits in the global work of CEF.

Returning home, Reese divided his time between KPI and CEF. Things at his plant were going well, but the same wasn't true for the ministry. In 1989, Reese had a phone installed in his Mercedes. It was one of the first car phones in Indianapolis and required a huge box in the trunk. He received a call from the man who had followed him as chairman of the CEF International Board of Trustees in Warrenton. Reese had spoken to him frequently about who should become the next president of Child Evangelism Fellowship.

"I know who the next president of CEF should be," said the friend. "It's you."

"Me?"

Reese laughed him off and for two weeks said nothing of the conversation. But the man called again and continued the drumbeat. At that point, Reese mentioned the matter to his prayer partners, one of whom replied, "Reese, it's obvious God has prepared you for this." When Reese brought up the matter to Linda, she gave her wholehearted support. She was ready to go, to give up everything, and to plunge into the work.

Reese flew to the CEF Board meeting in Anaheim, California, where he agreed to serve as the volunteer president for Child Evangelism Fellowship for one year, starting October 1, 1989. He left Anaheim for a long-planned teaching trip to Australia for CEF, and while there his term of service officially began. From the first day, things were difficult. He received a series of panicked calls from the States warning him that CEF was on the verge of a financial collapse, with problems stacking up like dominos waiting to fall.

Returning from Australia via Indianapolis, Reese arrived jetlagged at the CEF International Headquarters to find the leadership team on the verge of a breakdown. It was the capital of gloom and doom. The staff was discouraged. The buildings were bare and dark and neglected. Reese's office was a dismal room with dark cork walls and a few old pieces of furniture. His secretary, Dorothy Whitney was skeptical about him, but quickly became a trusted advisor and helper.

Reese wondered what he had gotten himself into as he walked the dilapidated buildings. He was fearful at the thought of his upcoming year, and he sensed everyone was afraid of him. They saw him as a successful executive from Indianapolis coming in like a buzzard to clean house. Reese realized that as a Board member he had only known "approximately 12 percent of the real story," as he later put it.

As he drilled into the situation in Warrenton, he found things even worse than he had imagined, and he began letting the Board know the real story. There were hard feelings, personality conflicts, theological battles, and financial crises at every level. The buildings were leaking. Buckets dotted halls and rooms. The warehouse was empty. Suppliers no longer provided CEF with paper or printing materials. The presses were silent and the shelves empty. Reese gathered everyone in the chapel for a pep talk, but it was interrupted when the ceiling caved in right behind him.

But God gave him optimism and tenacity. "I saw the potential in the place and I deeply believed in the crucial ministry that went out from that center," Reese recalls. "The property in Warrenton held the promise of lakes and trails and beautiful buildings to use as instruments for training children's missionaries and coordinating a global task of reaching souls for Christ. The opportunities were greater than ever. We had a unique purpose with people already in place around the world—if we could only survive the current set of crises."

> ## "I saw the potential in the place and I deeply believed in the crucial ministry..."

Reese pondered how the ministry could have gotten into the sad shape it was in, and he knew the devil was behind it. Satan had done everything in his power to attack the work of reaching the most fruitful mission field on Earth—the hearts of children. It was a shock to Reese. He walked around assessing the near hopelessness of the situation and began dictating letters on tape to the Board, explaining the status of the ministry. He also reassured the staff he wasn't there to fire people or to clean house.

Then he did the obvious. Making a list of everyone he knew who could make a significant financial contribution to the work, he started calling friends one by one, some of whom were the very ones who had advised him to come to CEF. Reese said bluntly, "We need help." One of his closest friends came to see for himself. Reese showed him around. The accounts payable that day amounted to $155,000, and there was no way CEF could meet them. The friend sat down on the spot and wrote a check for $155,000. That was the first big gift that came in, and it instantly delivered the ministry from its creditors.

"I was only 46 at the time," Reese says. "I drove nice cars, wore nice clothes, and I lived a different lifestyle from most of our missionaries. But I sought to reassure the staff of my commitment to them, to the Headquarters in Warrenton, and to the cause of global children's evangelism. I asked God to give me a love for our missionaries, and He did so quickly and dramatically. God built a love for those people in my heart."

The Lord also gave the Kauffmans a deepening love for the Warrenton property. In those days, many people wanted CEF to move its Headquarters to Indianapolis, which is where Reese and Linda continued living for a time. But Reese saw the acres outside St. Louis as a once-in-a-lifetime legacy for any organization, blanketed as they were with fields and woods and lots of room for recreation, ministry, and expansion. The buildings, if repaired and restored, were perfect for a mission like CEF.

Reese, Linda, and five-year-old Bucky moved into a unit of two rooms in a building that had previously housed monks.

Linda put together a cookbook with recipes from CEF missionaries around the world, and profits from this project were plowed into the most visible areas of the Headquarters buildings.

Then came a special blessing. One Friday the clouds rolled in, bearing the gift of deep, deep snow. A glistening blanket covered Warrenton. CEF closed its offices, and the Kauffmans went out and built a huge bonfire on the front lawn. They brought out an ATV, tied a rope to it, and started pulling around a large tire. Calling the staff, they said, "Come on out! We're having a great time."

One family called another, and one person brought another. They made snowmen and had snowball fights. They roasted hot dogs over open fires and brought in lots of food. The staff had never before enjoyed the property like that. Now for the first time, it felt lighthearted and was a fun place for families. That day's snowfall marked a decided change of attitude and it went a long way toward restoring a sense of joy to the workers, both about their location and their vocation. It was as though a new set of attitudes had blown in with the snow, brightening spirits and turning the grimness of the previous months to glistening hope.

Nevertheless, the sense of strain was hard to eradicate. Each week, Steve Bates, the financial manager at the time, would pick up Reese at the St. Louis airport. Steve's eyes always betrayed his feelings. The moment Reese walked off the plane and saw Steve's face, he could tell whether Steve had good news or bad news. It was usually the latter.

"I often saw fear in his eyes," Reese recalls. "Steve was an exceptional artist who had illustrated many CEF resources.

Somehow, he had ended up in financial management. As we drove to the offices each week, he briefed me and by the time I walked into the building, I was saying to myself, 'How are we going to get through this week? How are we going to survive?'"

One day Reese hopped off the plane, dreading to see Steve. Stopping himself, he realized that week after week, he'd been asking himself, "How are we going to get through the week?" And every week, they had gotten through the week. Somehow the Lord had borne them along, day after day, and week after week. Many times Reese had thought there was no chance of survival, but the Lord kept getting them through one week after another. Reese felt his morale increasing. He knew God would bring them through. This wasn't a human-based ministry, after all; it was God's. He who had begun this work would carry it on to completion. The Lord had started it before Reese came and He would carry it on long after Reese was gone.

"It was vital to know and believe that," Reese says, "because the attitude of a leader spreads to every part of the work and to every partner around the globe. And as the weeks went by, I gradually became more confident and committed."

One incident in those early days helped confirm the decision Reese had made to move from manufacturing to ministry. In assuming the presidency of CEF, Reese had entrusted the daily management of Kauffman Products to his son-in-law and other trusted associates. But one day, the men from his plant called and asked, "Reese, would you be willing to go to a machinery auction in Detroit to buy a piece of equipment we need?" These machines cost hundreds of thousands of dollars. Auctions are high-pressure events, in which bidders must make major decisions in a split second, and Reese was the best equipped in the company for that kind of pressure because he had lots of experience.

He agreed to go. For a few hours he re-entered the world of business. He studied all the machinery being sold, waited through the auction for the piece needed, and placed the winning bid. It all came back with a rush. It felt great to be with leaders of commerce and industry again, back in the swing of his profession. It was as different from Warrenton as day is from night.

Back in Missouri, things were critical. CEF couldn't make payroll. Bills were piling up and the operations fund was drained dry as dust. In Detroit, money was no object and leaders made decisions like kids playing marbles.

"For one day I'd gone back into business," said Reese. "I found myself watching a crowd of successful people in expensive clothes, many of the men sporting young girls on their arms, eating in good restaurants, staying in five-star hotels, bidding hundreds of thousands of dollars on one machine or another. Then leaving that rarefied world, I boarded the plane to return to the trenches of CEF, where our work was underfunded and our weary workers were barely hanging on. It seemed tremendously unfair. But when I got on the plane, I turned to 2 Corinthians 1:8-9 and read: 'We do not want you to be uninformed, brothers and sisters, about the troubles we experienced in the province of Asia. We were under great pressure, far beyond our ability to endure, so that we despaired of life itself. Indeed, we felt we had received the sentence of death. But this happened that we might not rely on ourselves but on God, who raises the dead.'[77]

"Those verses were all I needed to restore my spirits. I thought to myself, *We're having some tough times, but I'm not despairing of life yet. The apostle Paul went through something far worse than we're going through. He even despaired of life. He was in the will of God and doing the work of God, but the pressures were about to crush him. Evidently he had been on the verge of trusting his own abilities and skills. But the pressures taught him not to trust himself but in God who can raise the dead."*

That emphasis has become the keystone of Reese's leadership. We go about the Lord's work by faith, and in every condition we must learn to rely on God who raises the dead. Without Him we can do nothing, but we can do all things through Him who gives us strength.

Armed with ever-replenished courage, Reese began making changes at Child Evangelism Fellowship. He replaced the executive staff with a senior staff and began arranging telephone conferences with leading Bible teachers. Gathering his staff in his office, he placed phone calls to leaders like Warren Wiersbe, Paul Dixon, and John MacArthur. Those calls became valuable times of input and training together.

During one such call, President Paul Dixon of Cedarville University told them, "I have never been to your facility, but we have learned at our school that the culture of the campus is vital to our students. We estimate that within three weeks, the students have absorbed our culture. If we want good students, we have to have a good culture—the appearance of our buildings, the landscaping of the grounds, colorful flowers, clean common areas, trash-free sidewalks. An appearance of neatness and excellence makes the students want to reflect the same."

Dr. Dixon continued, "Make sure your property is a reflection of the excellence you want in your overall ministry."

As Reese and his team hung up the phone, God's conviction fell over them like a blanket. They walked out to the Volunteer Center, looked at the rundown buildings and pot holed roads, held hands, and prayed earnestly for God to help them change the appearance of the place within two years. Though they had no money, they saw the need.

Within 18 months, CEF completely replaced over 723 windows, painted the buildings, repaved the roads, and changed the whole appearance of the Headquarters into a professional environment that presented a culture of excellence, one that was conducive and complimentary to the work they were seeking to do in the hearts of children around the world. Since then Reese has tried to have at least one project underway continually. There's always a project going on—it may not be big—to improve the facility.

"I've found it also improves the attitude of our staff, workers, volunteers, and guests," he observes. "Our facilities don't have to be fancy or glitzy, but things should be done the best we can do them."

At the end of his one-year unpaid stint as president of CEF, the Board asked Reese to continue another year, and another, then another. In the quarter-century since, Child Evangelism Fellowship has become his life's work. For four decades as a committee and Board member, then president, Reese Kauffman has sought to bring vision, courage, conviction, and organization to one of the greatest works in the world—reaching the most fruitful but forgotten mission fields on Earth and to bring a generation of boys and girls to hear the Good News of Christ and to be His disciples. For Reese and the CEF family, these have been years of hard work and decades of harvest.

CHAPTER 10

Decades of Harvest

According to Gigi Graham, Child Evangelism Fellowship had a role in bringing together her parents, Billy and Ruth Graham. Since CEF was incorporated as a national movement in Chicago in 1937, it's understandable that students from nearby Christian colleges like Wheaton and Moody Bible Institute would be involved in those early days, including, it would seem, Billy Graham and Ruth Bell. "As students at Wheaton," Gigi said, "they both signed up for a particular child evangelism project, and before leaving campus the men and the women were praying in adjacent rooms. My mom heard a guy praying in the men's group and thought to herself, That young man knows to whom he is praying. It was Billy. They had not yet met, but this made an impression on her."[78]

The story of Child Evangelism Fellowship abounds in serendipitous works of God that have touched millions of lives in unexpected ways—works that have united the hearts of men and women toward uniting the hearts of children with God. The far reaching and on-going work of CEF may seem overwhelming in size and scope, yet its means and methods are childlike in their simplicity. The ministries of CEF are channeled through a handful of effective strategies that have evolved in God's timing and with His blessings.

Good News Clubs and 5-Day Clubs

Good News Clubs were born in the heart of J. Irvin Overholtzer in the early years of CEF. He knew that training gifted children's missionaries and evangelists was the key to multiplying his efforts. He established local committees to organize volunteers to conduct weekly meetings for the purpose of teaching girls and boys the Bible, sharing the Gospel with them, and helping them gain lifetime exposure to Bible stories, memory verses, Scriptural truths, and worshipful songs. This network of weekly meetings has been the backbone of CEF ministry around the world. These meetings are called Good News Clubs because they are safe and happy places for children to hear the Gospel. Good News Clubs have been occurring virtually nonstop around the world for the better part of a century. The ministry of CEF has many components, but Good News Clubs are the centerpiece of the work. In 2014, 69,556 Good News Clubs were meeting all over the world each week. CEF also sponsors 5-Day Clubs during school breaks such as summer vacation, taking advantage of the opportunity to evangelize and disciple children for five consecutive days, often in backyards or community centers.

> **In 2014, 69,556 Good News Clubs were meeting all over the world each week.**

Currently, CEF reaches over a half million children in the United States through our various ministries, but that's just a fraction of the whole. Worldwide, CEF ministered in person to nearly 20 million children during the 2014 ministry year. About 200,000 children are enrolled nationwide right now in Good News Club ministry. In the decades since 1937, millions of America's children have come to know the Lord through these Good News Club and 5-Day Club ministries. God has used CEF to bring these children to Himself so He can fill the hole in their hearts and give them a foundation for life.

We tend to think most North American kids go to church. That may have been true in the past, but not any longer. Most seldom—if ever—attend church, which means when a boy or girl walks into a Good News Club or 5-Day Club they know almost nothing about the Lord. CEF gives these children an opportunity to learn about God and His Word. CEF is committed to working with local churches and making sure every child has access to a loving congregation. But for some children, their first and only regular connection with believers and with the truths of Scripture is a weekly Good News Club.

[Kids] seldom—if ever— attend church...

CEF Good News Club ministry focuses primarily on children at locations outside the walls of a church, although preferably in partnership with local congregations. Child Evangelism Fellowship goes where the children are. Good News Clubs meet in places such as community centers, apartment complexes, and classrooms. In earlier days, many Good News Club ministries were held in homes hosted by godly Christians. Now, Good News Clubs are often held at elementary schools. The first time a Good News Club was held in a public school was in 1960, and in 1985, the original Equal Access Act was signed into law by President Ronald Reagan (without any input from Child Evangelism Fellowship).

Efforts to maintain access to the schools led to a dramatic Supreme Court case in 2001. It started in 1996, when Stephen and Darlene Fournier asked the Milford, New York Central School District if they could conduct a Good News Club after hours in a local school. The Fourniers believed that children with parental permission should be allowed to gather just like children did in other after-school groups. When the school district refused, Pastor Fournier took his request to court, and the case wound its way through the judicial system until it reached the highest court in the land.

On June 11, 2001 Reese Kauffman was driving to a college in Clearwater, Florida when his phone rang; he learned that CEF had won the case in a six-to-three decision. The Supreme Court had granted Child Evangelism Fellowship equal access to school facilities for after-school programs—the same as other groups.

Since that day, Child Evangelism Fellowship has sought to help Christians across America take advantage of this constitutionally mandated freedom to go into the approximately 65,000 public schools with the Gospel. Immediately after the bell rings in the afternoon, children who have parental permission can go to a room at their school with their friends to hear a Bible story, a memory verse, play games, and sing songs. They can hear the Gospel along with an invitation to receive Christ as their Savior. Teachers and school administrators across the nation have reported the benefits of Good News Clubs in curbing bullying, improving the mental health of children, and strengthening families.

Though this has been the law of the land since 2001, many churches are unaware of it. We bemoan the secularization of our nation's schools, yet fail to take advantage of the doors God has opened for us. CEF provides training and tools, they have invested decades developing means and methods, and they can also help clarify things from a legal perspective. But local churches must embrace Good News Clubs as a part of their ministry in fulfilling the Great Commission in their own neighborhoods. Good News Clubs represent the single greatest evangelistic and discipleship tool for local churches across the land.

A few districts in our country have Good News Clubs in every elementary school, but in any given week most schools in America still have empty, unused classrooms just waiting for a Good News Club. If you feel a burden for involving your church in sponsoring a Good News Club, please contact Child Evangelism Fellowship. America needs the witness of the Gospel in all the nation's schools while the door remains open, for forces in our culture are fighting every day to reverse this opportunity and to deny our children the right to hear the message of Jesus.

The Wonder Book

In 1998, CEF developed a unique discipleship tool called *The Wonder Book* to enhance its Good News and 5-Day Clubs. It happened when Henry Aoun of the JESUS Film Project asked CEF to develop children's materials to offer North Africans who were lined up at ports in southern Europe returning home from trips.

When Reese expressed interest, Henry came to Warrenton and presented the need to CEF writers and editorial managers.

Two of them, Martha Wright and Lynda Pongracz, wrote *The Wonder Book* in three days, and it was soon available in Arabic and French for distribution within Europe. The title comes from the format of the book, which asks a series of questions designed to lead children to discover biblical truth—questions like, "Have you ever wondered who the one true God really is?"

About a year later, when Reese visited a major foundation in Florida, he took a French copy of *The Wonder Book*. A woman at the foundation showed it to her daughter, who could read French. As a result, the foundation asked permission to publish an English version, and millions of copies went out. *The Wonder Book* is now available in over a hundred languages, and millions of copies are in print. It might be the most unheralded bestseller in recent history.

> **The Wonder Book is now available in over a hundred languages, and millions of copies are in print.**

Truth Chasers Club

The remarkable success of *The Wonder Book* led CEF to develop a Bible correspondence program for children. On the back of the English version of *The Wonder Book* was a tear-out piece directing youngsters to write for more information about the Lord. The overwhelming response compelled CEF to create an entire ministry devoted to providing discipleship resources for children to receive through the mail. It's called the Truth Chasers Club. God has richly blessed this work, which is now based in a special wing of the CEF International Headquarters in Warrenton.

Individuals from the local area and across the nation gather every morning to volunteer in the Truth Chasers Club. The volunteers range from youth groups to couples and individuals spending their vacations serving in the ministry to retirees devoted to using their time to serve God. On any given day, up to 50 volunteers gather at Warrenton to open mail, check lessons, write encouraging notes to children who have sent in lessons, answer questions, and pray for requests.

> **The Truth Chasers Club has averaged 55,000 active students.**

In the past three years the Truth Chasers Club has averaged 55,000 active students, 330,000 lessons sent out and 10,000 series completed. In the same time frame over 6,500 personalized Bibles were earned by children ages 7 to 17 who completed two series of lessons. When a volunteer opens a lesson in which a child reports that he received Christ as Savior, a bell is rung and everyone in the room pauses to rejoice, just as the angels are rejoicing in Heaven. Last year, that bell rang over 3,000 times!

THE BIRDHOUSE

One night in Warrenton, I went on a prayer walk and I noticed a birdhouse. It was sitting on a pole in the yard near our Headquarters building. Not long afterward, I took Bucky out there—he was in high school—and I showed him that birdhouse. I told him I'd been praying for a building for our Truth Chasers Club. By the grace of God and in answer to my prayer, that birdhouse became a building. Several years later I took Bucky back and we walked into the building and over to where the birdhouse would have stood, and there we praised God for answered prayer.

"My love for this ministry really goes back to something that happened to me in childhood," says Reese. "I vividly recall seeing an offer on a cereal box for a Flash Gordon ring. By sending in a certain number of box tops I could acquire this treasure. I ate cereal by the bowlfuls, collected the box tops, filled in the form, and sealed my envelope. My mom walked with me down to the mailbox and lifted me up so I could post my letter. I thought my ring would come the next day, and I waited and waited. By the time it arrived eight weeks later, I'd nearly forgotten about it. But I've never forgotten the excitement of posting a letter and waiting for the reply. That's the way we want children to feel about our Bible lessons—although we don't want to keep them waiting eight weeks for their response!"

Wonder Devotional Books

Though it is the goal of CEF to reply promptly to every child's letter, there's an inevitable lag time with the postal service. As CEF leaders considered this, they felt a growing concern for children who had no other access to the Gospel except by correspondence through the mail. "We wanted them to have more than a letter from us every week or two; they needed a word from the Lord every day," explains Reese. "So we pulled together our team to consider how to disciple kids on a daily basis. Out of those sessions came *The Wonder Devotional Book*, which provides 365 days of devotional material for children.

"Sometime after we started publishing *The Wonder Devotional Book*, I visited our works in Angola. I was taken to 15

Good News Clubs in a single day, dropping in on one, traveling to the next, and so forth. The lessons that day were from the book of Esther, and in each venue I saw hundreds of children studying this story. The youngsters were like sponges. They knew the answers, all the characters, the songs, and memory verses.

"The children were barefoot and barely clothed, most of them just wearing shorts. They had a 90-minute Bible exposure once a week, and my heart overflowed with gratitude. But as I visited these clubs, I felt the Lord say, 'We've got to do more for these kids. One lesson a week isn't enough. They need input from God's Word each day.'

"Returning home, I realized children everywhere need daily discipleship. *The Wonder Devotional Book* was too expensive and bulky to print and distribute around the world in its full form. So we published a booklet with the first 60 days and did a test run of a quarter-million copies in both English and Portuguese. The trial run was a triumph, and now we're sending out millions of these books all over the world in many languages—enabling children around the globe to learn God's Word each day."

> **"We're sending out millions of these books all over the world in many languages—enabling children around the globe to learn God's Word each day."**

In America and overseas, when children receive their own copies of *The Wonder Devotional Book*, they write their names on the bright covers and have a set of daily devotions to nurture them between weekly Good News Club meetings or periodic correspondence lessons. God has allowed CEF to provide millions of books to children around the world. In some cases, entire families are being won to Christ and discipled through Wonder Devotional Books.

In the day of Internet access and email, is there still a need for postal ministry and print products? Yes—there are few things that thrill a child like getting a letter or a book in the mail. But times and technologies are changing, and resources are also available on Wondersurf.com, an online ministry of CEF, which is packed with interactive lessons, games, songs, stories, videos, devotions, and activities. With a click of a button, almost any child anywhere in the world can learn about Christ at any time.

"What Went Wrong?"

Around the world, CEF missionaries have a deep burden for youngsters who have a parent behind prison bars. "Our ministry to the children of America's prisoners began when my brother-in-law, John Politan, was flying to the opening of a new golf course in Sedona," Reese says. "Several well-known Christians were on the plane, and John prayed that morning for an opportunity to be used of the Lord. On the flight, he sat beside Jerry Wilger, who asked him, 'Do you happen to know where I could get some evangelistic materials for children?'"

"As it happens," John replied, "I'm going to be speaking at a CEF conference next week in New Mexico."

That set in motion a remarkable chain of events. Jerry and Glenna Wilger, a successful independent business couple who worked with Prison Fellowship®, were burdened for the millions of children with one or both parents in prison. These children have a high likelihood of going to prison themselves. When a parent is arrested—sometimes in full view of the child—it devastates a youngster and creates an environment in which that child is severely at risk.

Hearing all this, the CEF leadership team knew they had to find a way to enroll these children in the Truth Chasers Club so they could hear the Gospel. Shortly thereafter, Jerry took Reese to Newton, Iowa, to visit a penitentiary and to see programs sponsored by Prison Fellowship. This was a new experience for Reese. He had never been to a penitentiary and was nervous, especially after Jerry asked him to speak to the inmates. The warden met them, and her words did nothing to calm Reese's nerves. "They don't want to hear you or hear about your God," she said, "but I will get them together and you can talk to them."

The inmates gathered in the gymnasium and someone handed Reese a microphone. He didn't know what he was going to say but, asking God for guidance, he told the inmates: "I don't know if you want to hear about my Lord and Savior Jesus Christ, but one thing is sure. You don't want your children in here with you, do you? You don't want that little boy or girl you love to be in prison, do you?"

The room became as silent as a tomb. Reese went on to tell these inmates that their children were at risk. There were already many father-and-son combinations in the system. Reese told them CEF was developing a program called "What Went Wrong?" which was designed to share the Gospel with inmates and to warn them of the dangers facing their children. It also gave the inmates an opportunity to enroll both themselves and their children in the Truth Chasers Club. Both the child and the inmate were sent an age-appropriate lesson.

As all this was unfolding, the CEF National Conference convened in Asheville, North Carolina. Jerry Wilger flew in to speak to the delegates about the plight of the children of America's prisoners. Though CEF was developing its "What Went Wrong?" program, there was no actual open door to any prison anywhere. As Jerry and Reese sat in rocking chairs outside the conference center, they prayed for God to somehow get them into the prisons.

Shortly afterward, the Secretary of Correction for New Mexico invited Reese to speak at the state's annual wardens meeting. They gave him one hour. Jerry and Reese filled up the time talking about the desperate needs of children of those locked up. At the end of that message, the Secretary of Corrections came to the podium and said, "We need this program in all our prisons. In fact, I mandate it right now." Turning to the men, he said, "Reese, as of right now you have the right to go into every prison and every cell in this state."

That opened the floodgates. Across the nation CEF now has more opportunities than it can fill. Not long ago Reese spent a day on death row in Texas and found inmates eager for our Gospel lessons for themselves and for their children. State after state has opened up, making CEF missionaries feel like the apostle Paul when he said, "...for a wide door for effective work has opened to me" (1 Corinthians 16:9) or the church in Philadelphia, to whom Jesus said, "Behold, I have set before you an open door, which no one is able to shut" (Revelation 3:8). Those doors are prison doors, and they're normally shut—but the Word of God is not chained. It can penetrate the cells of the most hardened criminals and into the hearts of their most needy children.

(As of July 2015, the Truth Chasers Club discontinued offering lessons to adults, including inmates. The Truth Chasers Club continues to minister to the children of inmates.)

"I THOUGHT IT'D BE COOL TO BE A CRIMINAL"

He walked into the chapel, head shaved and arms heavily tattooed, and sat in the second row. He had a nice smile and seemed engaged as I began to share about the "What Went Wrong?" program. "When you were children, did any of you want to be a prisoner when you grew up?" I asked. He raised his hand. I thought he'd misunderstood, for I'd never before had anyone answer this question in the affirmative.

"You wanted to be a prisoner?" I asked.

"Well, not really a prisoner, but I thought it would be cool to be a criminal."

"What about now? Do you still think that?"

"No."

"Do you have children?" I asked.

"Yeah, my son's in juvenile detention. We were involved in the same crime."

Looking at him, I felt a wave of sadness and asked him sincerely, "Would you like to try to keep your son from coming to the adult system?"

"Yes," he said. "I received Christ as my Savior two weeks ago and was baptized. I don't know nothing about the Bible, but I'm trying to learn, and I want to get my life together so that when I get out of here I don't come back. And I want to tell my son so that he can get his life together, too."

"I can help you," I said, and I went on to explain how the little booklet he held in his hand had an enrollment form so he could enroll himself and his son in the Truth Chasers Club. They would both receive free age-appropriate Bible study lessons by mail. By doing the lessons, they could learn what the Bible is about and how God wants us to live. If we had prepared these materials only for this man and his son, it would have been worth the effort.

–Debbie Walsh, Director of Prison Ministry,
Child Evangelism Fellowship

Other Ministries in the U.S. and Overseas

In recent years, the Lord has given Child Evangelism Fellowship many other ways to minister to children. One phase of the work is designed to children in military families. CEF also has a Camp Good News program. Missionaries and volunteers also conduct an annual Good News Across America outreach that targets a different city each year for evangelistic blitz. This type of outreach has been taken to other countries as well.

CEF also mobilizes in times of natural disasters or national emergencies to distribute a booklet for children and their families entitled, *Do You Wonder Why?*

That's not all. The Children's Ministries Institute that Jesse Overholtzer began many decades ago is thriving. CMI is a 12-week course offered at Warrenton and in locations around the world. Many of these classes are also available online. Through

CMI, CEF provides thorough, intensive instruction in children's work and evangelism.

To sustain these ministries, CEF needs a growing army of volunteers with biblical zeal for reaching children. This book is an appeal for your involvement. There's no way to calculate the ways God can use us as we lift high the cross of Christ and bring the message of Jesus Christ down to the level of a tender child. God has opened doors to America's schools, prisons, military bases and children. Now let's open our own hearts to embrace these opportunities for Christ and His children.

THE SIGN IN THE WINDOW

One of my first memories is of going to church on Easter Sunday when I was four. Our family seldom attended church, so I knew this was a special day. I loved it there and didn't want to leave. But I don't remember ever going to church as a family again, and I learned no more about God until I was in fourth grade. A neighbor lady, Mrs. Canzone, had a sign in her window that said, "Good News Club." I went to Mrs. Canzone's house, sat in her living room, and listened to the story of Jesus.

I ran home from the Good News Club, locked the door of the bathroom, and knelt in prayer. I asked Jesus to be my Savior. When I told my parents, they said to write a letter to my grandmother and she could explain more about Jesus to me. That started a tradition of writing a letter to my grandmother every Monday, which I did until her death 30 years later. Through letters and visits, my grandmother taught me to pray and to trust in God's care.

I needed those lessons years later when my husband was killed in a wreck on Christmas Eve. A woman committed suicide by driving head-on into our car. From the moment I opened my eyes, strapped to a stretcher beside the road, I remembered what I'd learned in Good News Club and from my grandmother. Jesus would never leave me or forsake me.

I was a widow and single mother for the next 16 years until the Lord brought another man into my life. Today my husband is a pastor, and our church supports Good News Clubs in our local schools, one of which my daughter currently attends.

And by the way, I still stay in contact with Mrs. Canzone.

–Joni Sobels[79]

As thankful as we are for our North America ministries, most of our work is international, with eight regional directors leading the work among the 194 nations where Child Evangelism Fellowship currently has active and sustained ministry. The exciting thing is that 94 percent of the approximately 2,900 people who serve with CEF around the world are national missionaries, serving and reaching children in their own cultures. Because they work in their homelands, they seldom face language or political barriers that cross-cultural missionaries face. It's often safer for them, especially in nations hostile to the Gospel.

The most extensive training vehicle of CEF, the Children's Ministry Institute, is training missionaries in at least 18 different locations around the globe. Through these CMI opportunities and other on-site educational programs, the ministry trained over 340,000 individuals in 2014. The majority of these teachers go back to their churches, schools, and other ministries with a better knowledge of child evangelism and honed discipleship skills.

> The exciting thing is that 94 percent of the approximately 2,900 people who serve with CEF around the world are national missionaries, serving and reaching children in their own cultures.

Richard Acquaye is one of the CEF regional directors in Africa. Richard began as a CEF volunteer in 1971 and began working full time in 1976. Today he oversees work in 23 countries. Richard's adventures sound like a movie script. Recently he landed in a particular country and wasn't allowed to leave the airport for five days. During that time he led a Congolese man to the saving knowledge of Christ. That was God's agenda for him for that week.

Richard also tells of what happened in another nation under his oversight. A girl was invited by a friend to a Good News Club. She began attending each week. Her father was the local witch doctor. After three weeks, the girl's mother said to the CEF missionary, "Tell me what kind of concoction you've given my daughter. She's now a changed person."

The teacher said, "Let me show you our concoction." She brought out a Wordless Book and explained it to the mother and her three children. All four trusted Jesus as Savior, and now they're praying for the father to be saved. Elsewhere in this same country, several churches have recently been planted because of the evangelistic efforts of trained CEF missionaries.

CEF also endeavors to equip missionaries with the materials and literature they need. Missionaries in the United States are usually able to purchase their own materials—the visualized Bible lessons, flashcards, songs, and other resources. But many overseas missionaries don't have the money to purchase supplies. In 1999, Buzz Baker, a dear friend of CEF, launched a program called "Boxes of Books" to equip teachers in under-funded areas of the world with the best materials CEF has to offer—free of charge. n with a goal of sending a thousand "Boxes of Books" to teachers in developing nations, knowing each box would cost CEF approximately $50. In 2014, nearly 189,000 boxes were shipped around the world.

But all the numbers pale in comparison to the need. Horrendous atrocities are being committed against Christian children in North Africa, the Middle East, and the Persian Gulf. Some are being beheaded, crucified, abused, and slain. Some are being kidnapped and sold into slavery. The enemy is seeking to destroy the witness of the Gospel all over the world. Despite the zealous efforts of a courageous band of missionaries, the goal of having an active ongoing ministry in every nation of the world seems staggering. Can one organization like Child Evangelism Fellowship really go "Around the World in 80 Years"?

According to Isaiah 58, as God's people follow and obey Him, our righteousness will go before us and the glory of the Lord will be our rear guard. We will call, He will answer; He will send, we will go. According to Isaiah 58, He will guide us continually, satisfy our needs in a sun-scorched land, strengthen our frame, make us like a spring whose waters never fail, and we will be called the Repairer of Broken Walls.[80]

Both at home and abroad, Child Evangelism Fellowship is trying to repair a broken world by reaching the most exploding demographic on our planet, our children. Sometimes it's hard to comprehend the impact Christ is making and the results He has wrought since Jesse Overholtzer first began weeping for the evangelism of the children of the world.

What other organization on Earth has been blessed with ongoing ministries in nearly every nation, reaching the most eager responders in the world, evangelizing million and millions of people annually through the personal, face-to-face efforts of our trained missionaries, recording millions of salvations, and training hundreds of thousands of individuals in the Lord's church, year-in and year-out for the better part of a century?

What other organization is driving toward a dream of reaching 100 million children annually for Christ?

All of this came home to Reese Kauffman in 1990, shortly after he'd been appointed president of Child Evangelism Fellowship. He and Linda received an invitation to the grand opening of a new Word of Life Camp near Clearwater, Florida. CEF was one of 17 ministries that showed up for pre-opening events. Reese had the pleasure of meeting the legendary founder of Word of Life, Jack Wyrtzen.

"When I introduced myself to him," Reese recalls, "he knew my name already, for he told me that he used to go soul-winning with my grandfather in Times Square. One person after another, representing some of the best-known ministries in America, introduced themselves to me. I was the 'new kid' on the block, and I spoke with several Christian leaders I knew by reputation but whom I had never met.

"As Linda and I drove back to the airport, we realized that nearly everyone who met us told us a story of how Child

Evangelism Fellowship had impacted their lives or their organizations at some point in the past. Some came from homes that hosted a Good News Club. Some had friends working in CEF-related ministries. Out of the 17 ministries represented in the event in Clearwater, 12 leaders told us of a direct impact on their work by CEF.

"We left there with a new appreciation of the heritage and power of Child Evangelism Fellowship. But we also left a little bewildered because most of these people had lost touch with our organization. Some didn't even know we still existed. Linda and I realized a ministry as powerful as Child Evangelism Fellowship shouldn't be the church's best-kept secret. So I want to tell you as sincerely as I can: Child Evangelism Fellowship has more open doors than ever. The times are urgent, the challenges are great, and the work is vital. We have a goal of being in every nation on Earth. We have a dream of reaching 100 million children each year with the Gospel of Christ. We're grateful for our heritage but even more excited about our future. We've been assigned a great work, and we could do so much more if we had one more person—just one more—helping us reach Every Child, Every Nation, Every Day."

That person is *you*.

CHAPTER 11

Around the World in 80 Years

A FTER LABORING AS MISSIONARIES IN CHINA FOR MANY YEARS, JOHN AND BETTY McGHEE FOUND THEMSELVES IN DANGER WHEN THE COMMUNISTS TOOK OVER THE NATION IN 1949. John was arrested on charges of being a spy, and Betty was expelled from the country with the couple's five children. After waiting as long as they could in Hong Kong, Betty and the youngsters settled in Memphis, Tennessee. The FBI sought news about her husband, but at one point it appeared that John had been executed. Thankfully, it was a false report and John was eventually reunited with his family in Memphis.

That's where Betty became involved in Child Evangelism Fellowship; and when the McGhee family moved to Cincinnati, Betty started a Good News Club in the lower level of their home on Beechtree Drive. Directly across the street lived the Schubert family, and every week little Chuck Schubert and his brother and sisters ran around to the back of Mrs. McGhee's house, through the door and into a large room on the lower level.

"We'd sit on the floor on numbered pieces of construction paper," recalls Chuck, "and she told us Bible stories using flannelgraph. As a five-year-old, I loved her smile and her gray hair wrapped up in a bun. I was in her Good News Club until I was in the fourth or fifth grade. She taught us memory verses, songs, and Bible stories. Sometimes she told us fascinating stories about China. One day when she asked if any of us wanted to accept Christ into our lives, I said that I did."

Chuck Schubert was as truly converted as anyone could be. In school he proved to be a natural leader and a good student, and he decided on a career in medicine. Between his first and second years of medical school, he worked in a church-related camp and met Julie, a missionary kid from West Africa. They married and Julie's love for Africa merged with Chuck's interest in medicine. The newlyweds spent two months in Cameroon, fully expecting to become medical missionaries in Africa—but the Lord had other ideas.

Dr. Schubert was impacted by the ministry of civil rights activist and CEF advocate, John M. Perkins, who encouraged the development of faith-based health care centers around the country. As a young man, Perkins suffered racial injustice, but he came to Christ as a direct result of his son's conversion at a CEF Good News Club. Since then he has made use of CEF resources throughout his life as he determined to bring the grace of Jesus into impoverished areas.

Challenged by John M. Perkin's example, Chuck and Julie felt God calling them to move into one of the poorest sections of Cincinnati and to engage in medical ministry. Out of that experience, the Schuberts, along with two close friends, founded Crossroad Health Center, which has been offering hope and healing to urban Cincinnati for many years now.

In more recent days, Chuck and Julie have spent much of their time in Zambia, where they labor in a hospital in a rural area. "It's a 12-hour drive from the capital city," said Dr. Schubert, "unless we take a puddle-jumper to a dirt airstrip near the hospital. But we find the work tremendously fulfilling."

Just as they did in Cincinnati, Chuck and Julie live among those to whom they minister and have a particular burden for children orphaned because of the HIV/AIDS epidemic. "Our oldest son, Chad, has really jumped on this vision and feels called to be part of what God is doing in Zambia," said Dr. Schubert. "He and his wife Bree have developed an orphan care ministry. Our other two boys, Travis and Ryan, who are preparing to be engineers, are involved as well and faithfully encourage them with their work with the orphanage."

Today, Dr. Charles Schubert divides his time between Zambia, Malawi, and Cincinnati, where he is Professor of Clinical Pediatrics at Cincinnati Children's Hospital in the Division of Pediatric Emergency Medicine. He donates vast amounts of time to providing healthcare to children and to families in crisis, both in major hospitals and in charitable clinics like Crossroad Health Center. He has received many awards including the Martin Luther King, Jr. Humanitarian Award and the Local Heroes Award from the American Academy of Pediatrics Council on Community Pediatrics.[81]

Can this kind of miracle be reproduced in every nation on Earth? That's the burden of Child Evangelism Fellowship, and that's the vision of Reese Kauffman. "Both in business and in ministry," he says, "it's easy to get into maintenance mode, to just keeping things going, and that's a rut. We only provide effective leadership when we cast a vision. As Proverbs 29:18 puts it, 'Where there is no vision, the people perish.'"[82]

That's why in 2007, Reese Kauffman gathered the CEF regional leaders and suggested a renewed strategy to bring discipleship to children around the world, even in hard-to-reach areas. After praying about it for a week, they met again to set a goal that by God's grace CEF would have active evangelistic and discipleship ministries in every nation of the world by its 80th anniversary. Soon, CEF missionaries were sharing the vision: "Around the World in 80 Years."

As of this writing, there are 13 countries to go. Some seem impenetrable, but CEF is depending on Christ's promise that He is with us always, even to the end of the age (Matthew 28:20).

"This isn't just something we think is a good idea," says Reese. "This is something God has told us to do. We aren't just to lurch through the process of evangelizing the nations; we must be intentional about it. Jesus was so intentional about giving us the Great Commission that it's recorded in Scripture five times—three times on the evening of His Resurrection (Mark 16:15; Luke 24:46-49; John 20:21), a few days later on a hillside in Galilee (Matthew 28:16-20), and a few weeks later on the day He ascended into Heaven (Acts 1:8). Like Jesus, we need to be strategic and intentional in fulfilling His commission both at home and around the globe."

If you walk into Reese's office in Warrenton, you'll see a well-arranged room filled with models of ships; a polished desk; shelves of his favorite books and photos; and on the wall, a plaque bearing a quotation from John Haggai: "Attempt something so impossible that unless God is in it, it's doomed to failure." Those 14 words are the heartbeat of the CEF vision.

> **"Attempt something so impossible that unless God is in it, it's doomed to failure."**

Jesus said in His sermon on the signs of the times, "And this gospel of the kingdom will be proclaimed throughout the whole world as a testimony to all nations, and then the end will come" (Matthew 24:14). No single congregation or organization can fulfill the Great Commission by itself; it takes all of us working together. But Child Evangelism Fellowship is determined to do its part as, by God's grace, it aims to take the Gospel to every child in every nation on Earth.

PART 3

Jesus Christ and the Miracle of Child Evangelism Fellowship

Child Evangelism in the Bible

EUROPEAN DIRECTOR, GERD-WALTER BUSKIES, TELLS OF AKVILE, A LITTLE GIRL IN LITHUANIA, SEVEN YEARS OLD AND THE DAUGHTER OF AN ALCOHOLIC MOTHER. Because of her terrible situation at home, Akvile tried to kill herself. Though only seven, she attempted to hang herself at the end of a bunk bed. Her brother, Alvydas, found her and rescued her, and one of our CEF missionaries visited her in the hospital and shared the Good News of Christ. Akvile trusted Christ as her Savior. According to her nurses, a remarkable change came over her. She began eating and drinking, happiness came into her heart, and she went to sleep every night, tightly clutching her Bible. Her brother also came to know the Lord as Savior. Akvile and Alvydas were later adopted by a Christian family and are now working alongside CEF missionaries in Lithuania.

Reaching children like this has been the burden of CEF from the beginning. One day, while CEF founder Jesse Overholtzer was poring over the book of Ephesians, two verses struck him. The first was Ephesians 1:1, which says, "Paul, an apostle of Christ Jesus by the will of God, to the saints who are in Ephesus."

The other verse came a few chapters later, in Ephesians 6:1: "Children, obey your parents in the Lord, for this is right."

Overholtzer realized that when Paul wrote to the Christians in Ephesus and addressed them as "saints," he was including the children. Paul spoke to the children in the church just as sincerely and pointedly as he spoke to the other groups. They were among the saints—those who were faithful in Christ Jesus, and they had a responsibility to hear and live by the instructions he was giving. Overholtzer later wrote, "The children of the church of Ephesus who were old enough to read a letter or have it read to them were old enough to be evangelized and born again."[83]

The Bible is filled with verses about the importance of reaching and teaching children. Perhaps the premier passage on this subject is Matthew 18, where the twelve disciples asked Jesus who was greatest in the kingdom. The Lord placed a child in the middle of the group. "Truly, I say to you, unless you turn and become like children, you will never enter the kingdom of heaven. Whoever humbles himself like this child is the greatest in the kingdom of heaven."

Jesus went on to say, "Whoever receives one such child in my name receives me." And He added, "See to it that you do not despise one of these little ones. For I tell you that in heaven their angels always see the face of my father, who is in heaven."

But Jesus wasn't finished. He went on to tell His parable of the lost lamb. The shepherd left the 99 to look for the lost one. He searched until he found it and rejoiced as he carried it home. Jesus was clearly stressing the importance of child evangelism with His concluding words, "So it is not the will of My Father who is in heaven that one of these little ones should perish."

ENTERTAINING FOR ETERNITY

Nan McCullough grew up in a family that went to church because, she said, "It was a nice thing to do. It never really meant anything more to us." When a new set of neighbors moved in, Nan noticed something different about them. Their joy was evident. One day they invited her to come to a Good News Club, and she joined the neighborhood children for weekly meetings.

"One day," Nan recalls, "the story was about a broad and narrow road. It's amazing that today I can clearly remember that flannelgraph from 1955. I can still remember kneeling beside that couch with several other children, praying and inviting Jesus to come into my heart. I went home that day with a new and different interest in spiritual things that no one else in my family had ever had."

Throughout her adult life, Nan has made a difference for Christ in Washington, D.C., and throughout America with Campus Crusade for Christ (known as Cru in the U.S.); the Christian Embassy; hospitality workshops; evangelistic luncheons; outreach training for wives of congressmen, governors, ambassadors, and generals; and her involvement with Child Evangelism Fellowship. Her book, Entertaining for Eternity, shares her passion for entertaining people to reach them for Christ, just as she found the Lord in a neighbor's home during a Good News Club years ago.[84]

At the CEF Headquarters in Warrenton, a museum-like display features Jesse Overholtzer's desk, globe, and Bible. The Bible is opened to Matthew 18—the Bible's mandate for child evangelism. The page is literally worn through, for

Mr. Overholtzer so often studied and preached from Matthew 18 he literally wore the page out of his Bible—though not out of his heart. Overholtzer said, "Jesus here settles the mooted question of the age, as to when children should be evangelized. He used a little child as an example, and Mark 9:36 makes it clear that the child was very little, for it states that Jesus took him 'in His arms.' Now how old a child does a man take in his arms if the child is not his own? Not over six and probably not over four or five. Matthew 18:6 settles forever the question whether little children can savingly believe."[85]

The biblical emphasis on children's ministry isn't limited to one or two verses or chapters. The Scriptures are as full of children as a city park on a sunny day. The Bible says:

- CHILDREN CAN BE BORN AGAIN: "From childhood you have been acquainted with the sacred writings, which are able to make you wise for salvation through faith in Christ Jesus" (2 Timothy 3:15).

- CHILDREN CAN TRUST THE LORD: "I am reminded of your sincere faith, a faith that dwelt first in your grandmother Lois and your mother Eunice and now, I am sure dwells in you as well" (2 Timothy 1:5).

- CHILDREN NEED CONSTANT EXPOSURE TO THE SCRIPTURES: "...these words that I command you today shall be on your heart. You shall teach them diligently to your children, and shall talk of them when you sit in your house, and when you walk by the way, and when you lie down, and when you rise..." (Deuteronomy 6:6-7).

- CHILDREN CAN GROW IN THE TRAINING OF THE LORD: "Fathers, do not provoke your children to anger, but bring them up in the disciple and instruction of the Lord" (Ephesians 6:4).

- CHILDREN CAN BE DISCIPLED: "Train up a child in the way he should go; even when he is old he will not depart from it" (Proverbs 22:6).
- CHILDREN CAN RECEIVE THE BLESSINGS OF GOD: "...they were bringing children to Him that he might touch them... And he took them in his arms and blessed them, laying his hands on them" (Mark 10:13-16).
- CHILDREN CAN PRAISE THE LORD: "...when the chief priests and the scribes saw the wonderful things that he did, and the children crying out in the temple, 'Hosanna to the Son of David!' they were indignant, and they said to him, 'Do you hear what these are saying?' And Jesus said to them, 'Yes; have you never read, "Out of the mouth of infants and nursing babies you have prepared praise"?'" (Matthew 21:15-16).
- CHILDREN CAN OBEY THE LORD: "Remember also your Creator in the days of your youth, before the evil days come" (Ecclesiastes 12:1).
- CHILDREN CAN DEVELOP MORAL VALUES: "My son, keep your father's commandment, and forsake not your mother's teaching" (Proverbs 6:20).
- CHILDREN CAN SERVE THE LORD: Think of Miriam watching over baby Moses in Exodus 2:7-8, young Samuel serving at the Tabernacle in 1 Samuel 3, the little girl who witnessed to the Syrian military officer in 2 Kings 5:3, and the little boy who offered Jesus his lunch in John 6:9.

"WHAT'S HAPPENED TO JOEY?"

Some people don't think 2 Corinthians 5:17 ("Therefore, if anyone is in Christ, he is a new creation.") applies to children. But I believe children can have their hearts changed as completely as anyone. I was conducting a Good News Club when a boy named Joey, age 7, came to Christ as I gave the invitation. The next week he came back and his mother was with him. She said, "I wanted to attend this class and see what you are teaching my son."

When I asked why, she said, "He's a different boy. Every week when I ask him to take out the trash he sasses me. This week I asked him to take out the trash and he said, 'You do it yourself...' then he stopped and said, 'That's not how Jesus wants me to talk.' And he took out the trash without complaining. And every week I drop him off at Sunday school and he always comes home with a note from one of his teachers complaining about his behavior. But this past Sunday the note said, 'What's happened to Joey?' They said he was like a different person. I want to find out what you are teaching him."

Today Joey is an adult and still living for the Lord. His life was changed as an elementary child who heard the Gospel.

–Morris Erickson, CEF missionary in North Dakota[86]

The Bible's authoritative pattern for a child's life is bound up in the example of Jesus, whose childhood years are summarized in Luke 2:40: "And the child grew and became strong, filled with wisdom. And the favor of God was upon him." That's what God wants for every child.

Verse 52 adds: "And Jesus increased in wisdom and in stature and in favor with God and man." He grew intellectually (in wisdom), physically (in stature), spiritually (in favor with God), and socially (in favor with...man). Could we wish anything less for our own children?

Child Evangelism Fellowship has been criticized—even vilified—by an increasingly secular culture that tolerates almost everything except the Gospel of Christ. Along with churches and Christians everywhere, we're facing a growing tide of secular extremism that opposes what Christians have been doing for 2,000 years—simply sharing the Good News of Jesus with people of all ages. CEF missionaries regularly face opponents who say, "How dare you evangelize children! Influence their morals! Expose them to Scripture!" Some have sought to hinder CEF work by legal means. In some parts of the world the opposition is even worse—outright persecution and physical danger.

It's tremendously encouraging to realize that despite opposition, the number of children coming to Christ is greater than ever in history. The work of child evangelism has never been stronger around the world. Nevertheless it's easy to be frustrated by the irony of our times. The same society that criticizes us for seeking to encourage the spiritual life of children stops at nothing to influence these same youngsters with its own messages. Its philosophy pervades schools and curriculum. Its media bombards children with thousands of questionable ideologies. Its advertisers view children as a demographic to be exploited. Video games vie for the attention of our youngsters for hours each day. The marketing of products and philosophies to children is something the world does aggressively, and the impact on our youngsters is greater than we can imagine.

It seems strange—incomprehensible, really—that in a world where children are at risk there should be opposition to providing them with a message of hope and moral direction. Many churches have been intimidated into doing little more than telling a few Bible stories to children and teaching a few character qualities. Other churches focus on children simply to keep parents happy during the adult service. But children need the pure, open, full, wonderful message of Jesus and His Good News just like they need food, water, and fresh air. They deserve our wholehearted efforts on their behalf for the glory of Christ.

NOT JUST FOR CHILDREN

The Gospel is for everyone, of course; not just for children. One of our CEF missionaries in the Russian city of Kursk began receiving CEF Truth Chasers Club lessons through the mail from a seven-year-old boy. Every lesson was carefully done, mailed in, processed by our volunteer, and returned with a new lesson. But when Lesson 8 came back, the truth came out. That lesson asked the question: "Have you received the Lord Jesus Christ into your life? If so, when?" The handwritten response was: "Yes, I have just prayed to the Lord and done that." But there followed these words: "While I have been answering the lessons, I pretended to be seven years old. The Lord has showed me now that I need to write to you that I have been telling a lie. I am not a seven-year-old boy but a 71-year-old man. Please forgive me."

This man may have been 71 years old, but he came with the heart of a child and the Lord gloriously saved

> him. The same message that can change the lives of children is the same that transforms people of all ages.[87]

According to Reese Kauffman, "It's our obligation as parents, grandparents, pastors, Christians, and workers in the Kingdom to lead children of all ages to Christ for salvation and to teach them His Word. In no other field would you let a child grow up without training. Take soccer, for example. If we waited until people were grown to teach them soccer skills, we'd have few teams. We typically learn best as children, and that's why our educational system is striving to reach children at younger and younger ages. It understands that a young soul is impressionable, trainable, eager to learn, and moldable for life."

That's why some people in our society are appalled when we tell children about Jesus. They want to eradicate all elements of spirituality in our world, and that means raising children who are secular and are not evangelized from the beginning. But there's power in the blood, and only the blood of Christ can cleanse us from our sins.

Some people have said to Reese, "You surely don't talk to children about the blood of Christ, do you?"

Reese replies honestly, "Are you serious? Look at what children are seeing on television, on the news, and on their video games. These children aren't naïve when it comes to blood; they just need to know about the blood of Jesus that cleanses us from all sin. After 2,000 years, the blood of Christ has not lost its power. Jesus died and rose again to give us a new start in life.

That's a message we can share appropriately and tastefully—but share it we must!"

In the Gospels, Jesus once prayed, "I thank you, Father, Lord of Heaven and Earth, that you have hidden these things from the wise and understanding and revealed them to little children; yes, Father, for such was your gracious will" (Luke 10:21). It was God's pleasure to give us a message little children can understand. The Gospel is so simple and wonderful that you can go anywhere in the world, to any child in the world, and share it. You'll likely find an eager listener and a receptive heart. Christianity isn't something we achieve; it's something we receive. And children are the best equipped to receive it.

At Child Evangelism Fellowship, one of the culture points is making sure there is a clear presentation of the Gospel, unaffected by so-called political correctness or pressure. Wherever you find CEF missionaries in the world you'll find this conviction: if we give up the message of the power of the cross of Jesus Christ, our purpose for existing will vanish. God's work isn't for the fainthearted. As Christians, we're to remain as undaunted as the three Hebrew boys before King Nebuchadnezzar in Daniel 3, or as Peter and John before the Sanhedrin in Acts 4. Jesus minced no words when He said, "Whoever receives one such child in My name receives Me, but whoever causes one of these little ones who believe in Me to sin, it would be better for him to have a great millstone fastened around his neck and to be drowned in the depth of the sea" (Matthew 18:5-6).

Visitors to the International Plaza at CEF International Headquarters in Warrenton see a monument in the shape of a millstone affixed in the sidewalk. It's to remind us—friend and foe alike—of how fearful it is to hinder the spiritual potential of a child's heart. But, in contrast, the most wonderful experience in the world is providing children with a biblical and moral foundation for life, to set them on the right path, to encourage them to love and live for the Lord Jesus who died to give them eternal life, and to teach them to obey all the things He has taught us. As we do so, He is with us to the ends of the Earth, for His words ring down through the ages with unmistakable clarity and conviction: "Let the little children come to me and do not hinder them, for to such belongs the kingdom of heaven" (Matthew 19:14).

CHAPTER 13

Child Evangelism in the Home

N O ORGANIZATION CAN REPLACE THE ROLE OF THE FAMILY—NOT CHILD EVANGELISM FELLOWSHIP, OR EVEN THE CHURCH. In both the Old and New Testaments, godly dads and moms are given the primary job of raising spiritual champions. From the creation of the world, God ordained the family as His chosen environment for the nurture of children. Emotional and spiritual growth best occurs under the roof of a healthy home where children get a head start on life. The home is God's primary venue for evangelism and edification. The family is His chosen launching pad for stellar lives.

Most parents want to raise healthy and happy children, but life is busy and demanding; sometimes we underestimate the time we need to devote to our children. "I've been a very young father," says Reese, "and later in life when Bucky was born, a more mature father. Age and experience are good teachers, and I wish I'd known from the beginning what I know now about the joy of being a dad. When my older children, Michelle and Rocky, were young, I was concentrating on my business, spending most of my time and effort to get it started. We had devotions at night and we went to church, but I was inexperienced at fathering. Looking back, I think I was too strict and rigid as a dad.

"By the time Bucky came along, I was better grounded in my spiritual life and more confident in business. Bucky was five years old when I became president of CEF, and Linda and I brought him into our ministry from the beginning. He was a full partner, so to speak, in our work.

"There are no perfect dads or moms—just read the stories in Scripture about parents—but we must be led by the Spirit and establish a stability that only comes from our love for our spouse and a commitment to lead a Christ-centered life."

Today Michelle fills her time doing good for others. She's part of an organization that furnishes clothing and other necessities for young children who find themselves suddenly going into foster care situations. Rocky has a design firm in Grand Rapids, decorating homes and making them beautiful. His work has been highlighted in many magazines and books. Bucky and his wife, Whitney, live just across the bay from Reese and Linda in Florida.

Reese's burden for the children of the world begins with his own kids and grandkids. "Our own families are our greatest ministries," he says. "Every day Child Evangelism Fellowship is burdened for every child in every nation; but we naturally carry a special burden for those very children God has placed in our own family circles. As fathers, mothers, grandparents, aunts, and uncles, we feel a God-given obligation to do our best in raising our precious youngsters in the nurture and instruction of the

Lord. According to Malachi 2:15, a healthy home is God's premier environment for producing 'godly offspring.'"

This has been the position of Child Evangelism Fellowship from the beginning. Jesse Overholtzer wrote, "It is very significant that the Lord placed the responsibility of evangelizing the children in the home.... If the father and mother do not know how to lead their children to Christ, it is their duty to find out how.... I believe it was God's plan that we go to Heaven by families."[88]

We have a hint of that in Acts 16:31 when the apostle Paul told the Philippian jailer, "Believe in the Lord Jesus, and you will be saved, you and your household." Paul understood that entire families need the transforming touch of Jesus Christ. He wrote in Ephesians 6:4: "Fathers, do not provoke your children to anger, but bring them up in the discipline and instruction of the Lord."

The Bible verbalized this pattern as far back as Moses, who said in Deuteronomy 6:4-7, "These words that I command you today shall be on your heart. You shall teach them diligently to your children, and shall talk of them when you sit in your house, and when you walk by the way, and when you lie down, and when you rise."

In Revelation 1:12-20, Jesus walked among the golden lampstands, which represented the various churches of Asia Minor. In the same way, He walks through the rooms of a home when its occupants confess Christ as Lord, and love and study His Word, and share their faith naturally with one another in conversation. Our Heavenly Father especially wants to impart biblical truths to children in this way. He tells us to do so as we get up in the morning, as we go to bed at night, while sitting at home and while driving down the road. Posting memory verses on the refrigerator or hanging them on the walls is our modern equivalent for writing His Word on our gates and doorposts. Inevitably a Spirit-filled home will be a Scripture-filled and Christ-centered one.

> **Inevitably a Spirit-filled home will be a Scripture-filled and Christ-centered one.**

The job of being a godly dad or mom is a lifetime calling. "Though my family is grown," says Reese Kauffman, "my fatherly responsibilities haven't expired. I'm still obligated to talk with my adult children about the Lord; it's natural to do so. Even to this day my underlying purpose in talking to my children—and I talk to them often—is to point them to Christ and to encourage them in Christ. Whether we're talking by phone or in person, I try to sprinkle my conversation with reassurances from God's Word or with an encouragement to pray about this or that. When I finish my work on Earth, I don't want to have any regrets of having failed to model my faith to the children God entrusted to me. We have to show up in their lives, to be present. Parents need be with their children, and nothing else will do. The lack of investing enough attention early on results in serious problems later on. If we invest in our kids from birth, the results will last for eternity."

Having said that, some of our duties as parents may sometimes seem, well, less than heavenly. Reese recalls two ladies from his church who paid a visit as he and Linda awaited the birth of their son. The women, who were known to be wonderful mothers, told Reese, "We can't picture you carrying a diaper bag, but you ought to try it. If you will change the baby's diapers, it will bond you to the child."

Reese thought the women were overstating the case. But as he pondered their words he began to believe them, and when Bucky came along he started changing his diapers whenever he was home. Having a penchant for facts and figures, Reese kept a running tally of the total. On the first Father's Day after Bucky's birth, Linda gave him a trophy bearing the words "Diaper Daddy of the Year" for having changed 200 diapers. It's a little trophy with a baby on the top, which he keeps in his study to this day, although he admits Linda changed thousands of diapers to his hundreds.

The point, of course, isn't about changing diapers but about shaping lives. We must invest ourselves in our children, and we can't begin too soon. We should quote Scriptures to our children while they're still in the womb, take them to church before their birth, and pray with them from infancy. If we love our children when they're young, they'll be more likely to love us when we're old. And if we teach them to love the Lord Jesus when they're little, they're more likely to follow Him all the days of their lives.

Our children see us making a living, cooking meals, watching television, and working at our tablets and computers. But do they see us reading our Bibles, bowing our heads in prayer, engaging in our devotions, and attending to our spiritual routines? Children learn by example. Even though it's necessary to provide discipline, the primary attitudes in the home should be those described in Galatians 5:22-23 as the "Fruit of the Spirit": love, joy, peace, patience, kindness, goodness, gentleness, faithfulness, and self-control. The best way to raise joyful children is to be joyful ourselves; the best way to raise loving youngsters is to exemplify love in the home. When they see us treating others with kindness, they'll learn from our example. We can go a long way in teaching our children self-discipline if we practice self-control.

"Notice what your children enjoy," Reese says, "what they're good at, where their interests are—and pursue those things with them. Find out what intrigues them and take advantage of it. Share their hobbies. Tell them stories. Be creative. You don't have to be a Tolstoy or the Brothers Grimm to make up stories for your children. Just use your imagination, and spin them some tales that have morals and meaning."

Read Scripture to your children every night. That gives us the opportunity to teach youngsters the Bible in a way that's as natural as giving them a hug or tucking them into bed. Along the way, we're able to instill some priceless memory verses into their minds, even as Psalm 119:11 says: "I have stored up your word in my heart, that I might not sin against you."

Most of all, be alert to their questions about Jesus, Heaven, Hell, death, and salvation. Watch for those moments when their hearts may be open to receiving Jesus Christ as Lord and Savior.

These are the things that build relationships. It takes time, but we have to realize it doesn't really take any more time than not doing it. If parents don't spend time with their children in the early years, they'll spend the equal amount of time later in anxiety and frustration over them.

Don't forget the importance of family traditions. Pray with your kids, but don't forget to play with them too. Be gentle with them. Our home life should have customs based around holidays, vacations, and other things; there should be elements that are exclusive to us. These traditions bond and build a family in a way that transcends generations, creating precious memories that last for lifetimes.

Reese recalls, "Recently for my 70th birthday my daughter sent me a letter with 70 memories for which she was thankful. Many of these were bound up in the little actions that reflected the habits God established in our home. Let's find ways of turning actions into habits and habits into traditions—Christian customs that honor God on the home front, establish a legacy, and contribute to the spiritual well-being of those coming after us. Psalm 71:18 puts it well in saying, 'So even to old age and gray hairs, O God, do not forsake me, until I proclaim your might to another generation, Your power to all those to come.'"

And remember, all these efforts will succeed only if accompanied by much prayer. Reese often asks parents, "Have you prayed for your child today?" Most parents don't pray for their children in a consistent and intensive way. That's a terrible waste. The most powerful thing in the universe is a father and mother praying for their children, for James 5:16 says, "The prayer of a righteous person is powerful and effective."[89]

Pray for the salvation of your children and grandchildren, their walk with God, their protection from bad influences and bad company, and their safety. There are a million pitfalls for children, but we have a secret weapon in protecting them—a weapon we can only access on our knees. Model your prayer habits after Epaphras in Colossians 4:12: "Epaphras... is always wrestling in prayer for you, that you may stand firm in all the will of God, mature and fully assured" (Colossians 4:12).[90]

This verse tells us: (1) how we should pray for our children—with earnestness, like a wrestler; (2) how often we should pray for them—always; and (3) what we should pray for them—that they may stand firm in all the will of God, mature and fully assured.

You don't have to "wrestle" alone. Share your children's needs with your prayer partners. Reese and his prayer partners have prayed for one another's children by name for decades, and now they can look back and see a string of miracles.

Even if we do all the things suggested in this chapter, challenges will come. Parenting isn't easy, and none of us escapes some heartaches and worries along the way. But when we have a roof shingled with God's blessings, a home built on the foundation of His Word, and an atmosphere filtered by prayer, we can better deal with whatever problems may come. Only Heaven knows how many tragedies have been avoided or blessings gained because of the power of parental prayers. Admittedly, we can't control our children or grandchildren as they grow older, but we can influence them whatever their age and pray for them whatever their stage in life. We should never give up on these youngsters. The Lord loves them even more than we do and He can do far more than we can.

Here's a final word: The greatest thing we can do for our children is to love our spouses. Whenever possible, a good marriage is the greatest stepping-stone to effective parenting. When a man loves his wife and a wife her husband, it provides an unspeakable security for the child growing up in that home.

> ## Here's a final word: The greatest thing we can do for our children is to love our spouses.

Perhaps the next greatest thing we can do for our youngsters is to love and respect our own parents. The Bible tells us to honor our fathers and our mothers, and this is the first commandment with a promise attached to it (Ephesians 6:2). There's no expiration date on that command. The way we treat our parents is how our children will likely treat us; and when our children see us respecting the role of our parents and caring for them, it fashions their view of both love and authority.

At speaking events in recent years, Reese has told audiences, "I've been thinking about the brevity of life. When a young couple learns they're expecting a child, they get ready, prepare the nursery, get a car seat, set up the crib, and buy some little clothes. Before they know it, their little one is crawling, then walking, then going to school, then going out on a date, then leaving home. It happens so quickly. If you haven't started pointing them to Christ in babyhood, praying with them, bringing God into their minds as soon as they start thinking, and setting their view of life correctly, it will soon be too late. Remember what Paul told Timothy: 'I am reminded of your sincere faith, which first lived in your grandmother Lois and in your mother Eunice... From infancy you have known the Holy Scriptures, which are able to make you wise for salvation through faith in Christ Jesus...' (2 Timothy 1:5; 3:15)."[91]

Child Evangelism Fellowship is deeply committed to evangelizing the children of the world while they're young, wherever they are, using any and all appropriate means. Many of the world's children don't have the joy of growing up in a happy and holy home. CEF is committed to standing in the gap. Even where there are good homes and families and churches, Child Evangelism Fellowship can play a role by coming alongside with encouragement and evangelism.

But every missionary at CEF also believes the primary God-ordained place for spiritual nurture isn't in a Good News Club, a Christian school, a Sunday school classroom, or church sanctuary. All these have a vital role to fill. But there is no substitute for a Christ-centered home where our children can grow up like Jesus—in wisdom and in stature, and in favor with God and man (Luke 2:52).

SOMETIMES IT WORKS IN REVERSE

While parents are commanded in the Bible to evangelize, teach, and disciple their children, sometimes it works the other way. CEF European Director Gerd-Walter Buskies reports that the former head of the KGB (the Soviet-era secret police) in Ukraine was an atheist who was fiercely opposed to God, Christianity, and the Bible. His two small daughters nevertheless began attending a Good News Club and both eventually received Jesus Christ as Lord and Savior. The change in their behavior astounded their parents, who, despite misgivings, allowed them to begin attending Sunday school at a local church. Finally, the parents also began attending. One Sunday morning, the girls were astonished to see their father, the atheistic KGB leader, come to the altar, kneel down, repent of his sins, and give his life to Christ. Shortly afterward, the mother did the same.

CHAPTER 14

How to Lead a Child to Christ

WHEN CEF MISSIONARIES MARK AND ROXANNE SHINGLETON BEGAN A GOOD NEWS CLUB AT KHULANI HAVEN ORPHANAGE IN SOUTH AFRICA, THEY TOOK SPECIAL DELIGHT IN A YOUNG FELLOW NAMED THABO, WHO LOVED PLAYING SOCCER WITH MARK AND RELISHED BEING THEIR FRIEND. During a Good News Club in 2003, as Mark shared the message of *The Wordless Book*, Thabo and three others professed Jesus as Savior and Lord.

In the following weeks, Mark and Roxanne took some of the youngsters home for overnight visits to give them a few hours' respite from orphanage life. One week, Thabo stole some items from their home, but he confessed as to what he had done and began weeping. His tears endeared him even more deeply to Mark and Roxanne, and they watched with pleasure as he grew in the Lord.

Three years later, in October 2006, Mark and Roxanne attended a weekend youth camp near the seaside city of Durban. On Saturday morning, as Thabo played in the shallow water with his friends, a large wave struck, knocking two of the boys off their feet and sweeping them into deeper water. One of the boys, Fanie, 17, was rescued, but Thabo drowned.

Realizing how close he had come to death, Fanie gave his life to Christ the following week. At Thabo's funeral, 21 other young people received Christ as their Lord and Savior. Mark and Roxanne grieved for Thabo and his shortened life; but they are so thankful for the joy of leading him to Christ with *The Wordless Book* and for Thabo's influence, which is still at work in South Africa.

Child Evangelism Fellowship uses many tools and methods in sharing Christ with boys and girls, but throughout its history *The Wordless Book* has been at the forefront of its Gospel presentations. It is a colorful presentation of the world's greatest message, presented in a way everyone on Earth can understand.

The Gospel itself, though simple, is profound. The Creator-God who made the universe and imparted life to each person is pure, perfect, holy, and infinite. He revealed His glory in the universe He made and in the Book He inspired. The Bible describes God's perfect qualities and warns us we've all fallen short of His glory. Everyone has sinned and violated God's holiness, and that inevitably separates us from Him and from His eternal life. Yet God built a deep moral principle into His universe, that a sinless sacrifice can die in our place and restore us to fellowship with Him. God Himself became that sacrifice through Jesus Christ, who carried our sins, absorbed our death on the cross of Calvary, rose from the tomb, and made it possible for us to be reconciled with God. In Christ we have redemption through His blood, the forgiveness of sins (Ephesians 1:7). A restored relationship with

God provides a foundation of purpose and peace in life, as well as the assurance of eternal life forever in Heaven.

But how do we explain all this to children? CEF missionaries often do it in living colors with *The Wordless Book*. The Bible is filled with verses that contain deep truths of God's saving grace. *The Wordless Book* has been used as a primary witnessing tool by CEF missionaries because it uses simple colors to convey some of those deep truths. No one knows the origin of this tool, but it's usually traced back to Charles Haddon Spurgeon, whose influence seems to have had an outsized impact on the work now known as Child Evangelism Fellowship. In 1866, Spurgeon preached a sermon in which he described an old, unnamed minister who put three colored pages together and often looked at them to remind himself of his sinfulness, of Christ's blood poured out for him, and the cleansing provided.

> **The Wordless Book has been used as a primary witnessing tool by CEF missionaries because it uses simple colors to convey some of those deep truths**

A decade later, evangelist Dwight L. Moody used *The Wordless Book* during his 1875 Gospel campaign in Liverpool, England, adding a gold page to represent Heaven.

Shortly afterward, hymnist Fanny Crosby, author of "Blessed Assurance," used the *The Wordless Book* in America; and missionary Amy Carmichael did the same in India, where she referred to the colors as a "most useful text for an impromptu sermon."

Pioneer missionary Lilias Trotter, who labored for Christ in Algeria at the turn of the 20th century and whose writings inspired the hymn, "Turn Your Eyes Upon Jesus," wrote about an experience she had with *The Wordless Book*: "Soon I had a little congregation on the riverbank, looking at *The Wordless Book*, a tiny four-page volume that the illiterate women seem to understand. The gold page stands for Heaven and the glory of God, the dark page for sin that shuts us out, the red page for the blood of Christ which cleanses from sin, and the white page for a heart forgiven and washed clean."[92]

GOT ANY RIVERS YOU THINK ARE UNCROSSABLE?

When CEF missionary Marie-Marthe and her friend were trying to reach a remote village in Madagascar to train others in child evangelism, they were stranded by an unscrupulous taxi driver and told to go back where they came from. They soldiered on, determined to walk the remaining 20 hours to their destination. Then a man offered to take them on a motorcycle for $30. Up steep hills they went, over small rivers, down stony paths, and through mud until they reached a halfway point five hours later. From there it was on foot, which meant crossing a wide river infested with crocodiles. Marie-Marthe, who couldn't swim, waded into the waist-deep water. "I stepped on something soft," she said, "I didn't know what, but I just went on. And praise the Lord, I got across."

They hiked up mountains, down slopes, through valleys, and across rivers. "It was dark and we didn't even have a flashlight," Marie-Marthe said. "We were exhausted, but after hours of hiking, we reached the village."

The villagers were thrilled to see them, and that week Marie-Martha had a productive time teaching child evangelism principles to eager recruits and missionaries. Every afternoon she also gathered the children to explain to them The Wordless Book. As a result of that trip, hundreds of children came to know the Lord Jesus as Savior.

Today the colors of *The Wordless Book* show up in countless ways—on wristbands, handkerchiefs, lapel pins, face paints, and soccer balls. Using these colors, anyone can explain the Gospel in just a few minutes to a child or an adult. If you want to use the colors of *The Wordless Book*, here are some suggestions about what to say.

Show the gold page first, and ask, "What does gold make you think of? Treasure? Jewelry? Some people have lots of these. But the one who is richest and most generous is God. He owns the whole world because He made the world and the sun and the stars. He also made you and me. God lives in Heaven, a wonderful place of light, beauty and happiness. The Bible describes Heaven as having a street of gold. God wants you to go there someday and live with Him forever.

"But gold is also pure. This also reminds us that God is pure and holy. He has never done or said anything wrong. Because all of us sometimes do wrong things, we are not pure like God is.

"The dark color represents the darkness of sin, for the Bible says, 'All have sinned and fall short of the glory of God' (Romans 3:23). Wanting our own way is sin. Doing, saying or thinking bad things is sin. Sin is disobeying the rules God has given in His book, the Bible. Can you think of some ways we sin? Why is it so easy for us to tell lies, to lose our tempers or be unkind? Because every one of us is born with a sinful nature. Sin causes sadness in our world. Sin hurts others and it hurts you. It saddens the heart of God. That's why the Bible describes sin as darkness (Ephesians 5:8, Colossians 1:3), and living without Christ is like living in a world with no sunshine. Can you imagine a world where the sun never comes up? Without Christ, we are always walking in darkness (John 8:12). People love darkness rather than light because their works are evil (John 3:19).

"The next color, red, stands for the blood Jesus shed for us. The Bible says that even though we have sinned and live in spiritual darkness, God loves us. He loves you very much. God loves you so much He became a man—Jesus Christ—to die for you. Jesus died in a terrible way, by being nailed to a cross. Can you imagine someone loving you enough to willingly die for you? Jesus did that. The Bible says, '...the blood of Jesus his Son cleanses us from all sin' (1 John 1:7). Three days later Jesus came alive from the dead and now He lives in Heaven. He can take away the darkness of sin that separates you from God.

"Next is a clean color. This page reminds us that we can be clean and pure before God. When you receive Jesus Christ as your Savior, God will forgive you and make you clean from sin. Then, one day, you will live with Him in Heaven.

"The Bible says, 'For God so loved the world, that he gave his only Son, that whoever believes in him should not perish, but have everlasting life' (John 3:16). What does it mean to believe? Believing means turning to the Lord Jesus and trusting Him to forgive you and give you everlasting life. You must be willing for

God to help you stop doing wrong things and trust Him for forgiveness. Jesus promises He will forgive you. Perhaps you would like to do that today."

Having presented the Gospel in all its vivid colors to boys and girls, we never want to pressure children into trusting Christ as Savior or to create a situation in which a child makes such a decision just because others are doing so. It's vital to be sensitive to the leading of the Holy Spirit, knowing how and when to gently encourage each child individually, one by one. In our training, we encourage Good News Club teachers to ask these questions to children who respond and inquire about being a Christian: Why did you come to talk with me? Why do you need the Lord Jesus Christ? The way in which children respond to those questions gives us clues as to how to proceed.

Children will come to the Lord as He leads them, without any coercion from us. We can provide the wonderful message along with gentle encouragement and clear opportunities, but it's the Lord who works in their hearts.

If the child truly desires to put his faith in Christ, without coercing him, you might say, "Are you willing to turn from your sin and believe in Jesus as your Savior now? If you are, you could tell God something like this: 'God, I am sorry for my sin. Thank you for Jesus who died for me. Please, help me to turn from my sin and forgive me. Please, make me clean.' If you trust Jesus, God sees you as clean and pure because of His Son."

But wait! There's one more page. The last color is green, which stands for growing in Christ. We tell children, "Green is the color of grass and trees and of things that grow in the garden and park. You're growing too—taller and stronger each day.

When you become a follower of Christ, you want to begin growing spiritually. We grow strong on the inside as we read the Bible and pray each day, as we memorize and think about His Word, and as we gather with other Christians to worship Him. We also grow as we tell others how good God is and what He has done for us.[93]

NEVER SPEECHLESS WITH A WORDLESS BOOK

Terri Futo tells of meeting two 91-year-old women. Polly, who was at her daughter's home, was afraid to die because she knew she was not good enough to go to Heaven. Agnes, who lived in a nursing home, was certain she was good enough to go to Heaven, though she had never given her life to Christ. "Using the training I received through Child Evangelism Fellowship," Terri said, "I was able to present the Gospel in a simple loving way just as we do to children. Oh, it was very evident that they had understanding as they each received Jesus as Savior. Both had joy and peace that they did not have before."

It's important to use God's Word to give children assurance of their salvation. As children receive Jesus Christ as their Savior, it changes the direction of their lives for good, and it can save them from a lifetime of personal emptiness and moral failure. It also reassures them of eternal life in Heaven, which is very important in the heart and mind of children. Jesse Overholtzer once pointed out the importance of telling children about Heaven. "We have found by years of experience that the message of Heaven, if properly presented, has the strongest appeal to a child. Heaven should be described, in simple language, as the last two chapters of the Bible tell about it. A loving God, preparing such a wonderful place, just for us, and the fact that He wants all of us to be with Him there, touches the heart of a child very deeply."[94]

CEF missionary Sue Richards had a boy in her class who sat near the back and never responded. Sue didn't think he was listening at all, until one day when she went through his workbook. One of the questions said: "If Jesus asked you to follow Him, what would you say or do?"

The boy had written, "I would hit Him over the head with a hammer."

The front of the book was violently scratched, apparently with a knife. Sue couldn't help wondering if he'd end up in trouble. He seemed to have all the marks of rage and anger. Deeply burdened, Sue approached his teacher.

"There's nothing more we can do," said the teacher. "The police are involved, the principal, the psychologist, everybody. Nothing can be done with this boy."

Sue disagreed. She recruited her mom as her prayer warrior, and she carefully confronted the boy with his statement about hitting Jesus with a hammer. "I've seen what you have written in your book," she said. "Do you want to talk to me about something?"

No. He did not.

"Is everything all right?"

"Yep."

"Well," said Sue, "I just want you to know one thing. I am not paid to be here like the other teachers. I am a Scripture teacher.

I am only here because I love you; because Jesus loves you. He died for you. And your life doesn't have to be like this."

That's all Sue said to him, but the next week his book was open and he made eye contact with her. It was a Christmas lesson, and Sue asked the children to use the letters of the word *Christmas* to write down what Christmas meant to them. She was astounded when she saw his answer. He had written: "Christ has returned in spirit to me and saved me."

Later, Sue was able to speak to the boy's mother, who was battling addictions. "Yeah," said the mother, "I don't know what's gotten into him. He's gotten all religious all of a sudden."

But it wasn't religion; it was Christ. Whether with *The Wordless Book* or some other way of explaining the plan of salvation, ask the Lord to give you the opportunity to share the Gospel with a child. Millions of youngsters around the world are just waiting for someone to tell them, "Your life doesn't have to be like this. Jesus loves you. He died for you. He has a wonderful plan for your life and you can become His follower here and now." Some of them will do so; and their family and friends won't know what—or who—has gotten into them!

PART 4

Biblical Convictions and the Ministry of Child Evangelism Fellowship

CHAPTER 15

Leadership

D URING HIS 25 YEARS AT THE HELM OF CHILD EVANGELISM FELLOWSHIP, REESE KAUFFMAN HAS TRAVELED THE WORLD SPEAKING ON CERTAIN THEMES THAT ARE DEEPLY EMBEDDED IN HIS HEART. The closing chapters of this book will spotlight some of these Kauffman convictions. Those who have heard Reese speak will hear his voice coming through in these pages, which are devoted to the themes of leadership, giving, prayer, and enthusiasm.

The book of Proverbs says, "When the country is in chaos, everybody has a plan to fix it—but it takes a leader of real understanding to straighten things out" (Proverbs 28:2).[95] The story of Child Evangelism Fellowship has included some chaotic periods, but God has always raised up leaders with enough understanding to straighten things out. As we've already seen in prior chapters, the history of CEF isn't just a matter of events and dates, not even a matter of fire and fervor and unforgettable missionaries. It's a matter of leadership. And what is leadership? It is *vision* plus *supervision*—the ability *to dream* and the capacity *to do* and *to direct*.

It takes a unique individual to personify both vision and supervision, but that's the way God trained Reese Kauffman. He is a Christian businessman who speaks the language of high volume manufacturing, can read financial statements as easily as he can the comics, can seal a deal with a handshake, and can shake up an organization when needed.

> **And what is leadership? It is vision plus supervision— the ability to dream and the capacity to do and to direct.**

Reese evidenced an aptitude for these skills early in life. Once when he was young, for example, Reese appointed himself leader over his siblings. Every night he pretended to blow a military horn and shouted, "Attention!" His sisters took that as their cue to get into bed and move their legs as though marching. Left, right, left! At the end of the drill, Reese announced which of them would tell a bedtime story while the others listened in their beds—the girls in their bedroom and Reese next door in his.

Since the girls didn't like telling stories, the task often fell to Reese, but his stories were too long, and the sisters had a penchant for falling asleep in the middle of them. So Reese found a way to keep them awake. He tied a string around the big toe of each of the girls and extended the strings to his bedroom. When he suspected they had fallen asleep during one of his stories, he gave the strings a yank to wake them up.

"In the years since," Reese says, "I've learned that good leaders don't need to pull strings or manipulate people like marionettes; the quality of their command comes from the strength of their character. Effective leadership depends on certain tools, which, at their essence, are biblical habits built on God-given gifts."

Faith

Reese's most important tool is the fulcrum of faith. That's what keeps all the other elements balanced and tilted toward the Lord. Faith is a weapons-grade ability to trust the Lord with the ups and downs of lives and organizations, and with the problems that come, and with the potential of the work. We don't just live by faith; we lead by faith. One of Reese's favorite verses about leadership is Proverbs 29:26: "Many seek the face of a ruler, but it is from the Lord that a man gets justice."

"Take this verse into a business setting," Reese explains. "A ruler is someone with influence inside a company. Leaders are decision-makers who can help businesses and organizations thrive. We seek face time with leaders because we think they can do something for us. Perhaps we want their business. Perhaps we need their influence. But as we do so we must remember that the Lord is the One controlling the process and granting the results, which allows us to approach the enterprise with a sense of Godward faith. For example, in business I would work for a month to get 20 minutes with someone to whom I wanted to present our company, but I learned I had to trust God for the results.

"Our confidence and morale doesn't really reside with the leader but with the Lord. We do have to seek these people out—that's the way the marketplace is built—but God controls the rulers. God gives out the business. God moves the hearts of ministry partners. God brings the customers. God is the source. So it's the fear of God that should drive and encourage us—not just the person with whom we're trying to connect.

"We have to trust God's direction. A true leader is a man or woman of faith. They learn to trust God with the ins and outs of the business climate and with the problems and potentials of their work. They do their best, seek His face, and leave the results to Him. Perhaps that's the reason I don't dread problems. I love them—or at least I appreciate the fact that problems are things to be solved, improvements waiting to happen. A good leader looks forward to solving problems in a way that will push the enterprise forward."

Love

Genuine leaders also need the wheel of love to keep the work rolling effectively. Reese believes leaders should exhibit an unnatural, supernatural love for those whom they lead. Knowing that it's much easier to lead someone we love than someone we merely tolerate, Reese regularly offers this prayer: "Lord, help me love the people of CEF. Give me a tender heart for them."

This servant leadership shows up at the most unexpected times. For decades now, the Kauffmans have circled the globe on behalf of CEF, and remarkably neither Reese or Linda or their son Bucky has ever had a bout of traveler's sickness. That's partly because they're cautious about what they eat, especially in developing nations. Once in an African country they were entertained by a wealthy family. The man was an architect but a non-Christian. The woman was a Christian. The family had comfortable guest quarters with workers to attend to the affairs of the household.

On the Kauffmans' last night there, two of the servants brought supper to their room. It was a beautiful salad, and much care had been put into its preparation. It was arranged on a plate like an elegant painting. Reese thanked the workers and took the platter, then wondered what in the world to do with it since they don't eat unwashed vegetables or raw food overseas. They knew the salad, beautiful as it was, was unsafe for their digestive systems.

"Let's flush most of it down the commode," Reese suggested. "We can mess the rest of it up as if we had eaten it."

"We can't do that," Linda said. "That's not really honest. Plus, it'll end up in the open sewer that runs right in front of the house and they might see it."

The salad ended up going with them in their luggage. They disassembled the lettuce and raw vegetables, wrapped them up in plastic bags, packed it in their suitcases among shirts and suits, and disposed of it when they arrived in London. They obviously couldn't tell their hosts they had eaten the salad, nor did they tell them they had packed it among their dirty clothes. But they could honestly tell them they appreciated their thoughtfulness, and they did so in a way that conveyed love and respect.

Loving others requires constant sensitivity. Reese readily admits he's not always as sensitive as he ought to be. "The biggest problem I have with Child Evangelism Fellowship is the man sitting in the chair behind my desk," he says. "Like most people, I struggle with pride, self-centeredness, and ego. If you've read *The Calvary Road* by Roy Hession, perhaps you remember his point about shyness being a form of inverted pride. I've had to struggle with this. Pride and ego are the number one enemies for a leader. If you can handle those two issues, you have a much greater opportunity to succeed.

"I think the greatest problem for those men who fall into sexual sin (and perhaps women too) is ego, not lust. I once spent a day counseling a friend who was determined to divorce his wife. He admitted that his wife was far more beautiful than the woman with whom he was developing an illicit relationship. But the other woman had built up his ego.

"Leaders are accustomed to having their egos stoked and stroked. This is a battle for us. On the one hand we want to use the gifts and talents God has given us. If you're a leader, you want to come out and rally the troops and inspire them with your vision and agenda. But on the other hand, you often fall into the trap of wanting to be esteemed."

"Because of my frequent travels," Reese says, "I'm often bumped into first class with big shots and executives. That's a danger zone for me. Perhaps I've worked hard for the Lord all week, and on my way home I'll start talking with these first-class people who tend to brag a bit. A subtle competition comes into play, and during the conversation I'll talk about my boat or my travels or my car or my house. I tend to exalt myself. After I've worked all week to be a humble servant, I get on a plane and speak boastfully. By the time I get home I feel rotten about myself.

"We have to remind ourselves we're nothing except servants of God whom He wants to use in the ways He has planned for us. Though we will never completely understand our infinite God with our finite minds, our view and knowledge of Him must constantly expand. It reminds me of the shape of a funnel that is smaller at one end and widens at the other end. Every day our concept of God should widen as we see Him in His creation, in

His work, and in His Word. Every day I pray, 'Lord, help me see Your hand today at work.'"

Reese's favorite Bible character is David, who is the second character in Scripture in terms of amount of space devoted to him, behind the Lord Jesus. Sixty-six chapters are written about David in the Bible, and he's mentioned 59 times in the New Testament. David wasn't perfect but he had a heart for God; he was a man after God's own heart. Even after his failures, he always came back to God. He's an example of wholehearted devotion.

"You can't lead without that," says Reese. "You have to love the Lord before all else, and that love must translate into graciousness and concern for those with whom you labor. They have to constantly sense that the love of God is being shed abroad in our hearts."

Several years ago, Reese was invited to Jamaica to speak for CEF. He was asked to teach a course on interpersonal relationships. From there he went to Africa and delivered the same material. In both Jamaica and Africa, everyone listened with interest, for the missionaries were all struggling with their relationships with each other. Then he attended the European CEF Conference. This was shortly after the fall of the Iron Curtain, and for the first time CEF missionaries from Eastern Europe were able to join the Western Europe staff. They asked Reese to speak on interpersonal relationships. The room where he spoke was so packed he had trouble getting through the door. He was astounded because he knew the Eastern Europe missionaries had suffered for the cause of Christ. Many had endured persecution under Communism. Reese assumed they had developed a level of maturity that wouldn't need anything he could say to them about interpersonal relationships. But he found they had the same problems as the people in Jamaica and Africa.

"One of the biggest challenges of Christian work is getting along with our coworkers," Reese admits. "This is true among Christian colleges, churches and church staffs, and ministry organizations. When I came to CEF, I came out of a manufacturing operation with all kinds of people working together in an organized system toward the same goals. I thought Christian work would be the same. I thought everyone at Child Evangelism Fellowship would be walking down the halls singing hymns all day. But I was amazed to discover the human resources division at CEF had more problems than the human resources division at my factory in Indianapolis.

"In Christian work, we have a great adversary. It's easier to run a business than a ministry, because a business doesn't have the adversary attacking its unity. This is why Jesus specifically prayed in John 17 for the unity of His followers. When the devil attacks the unity of the body of Christ, he is attacking the deity of Christ. Jesus Christ was the only begotten Son of God, and His identity is reflected by the unity of His followers. When the devil attacks the workers of a ministry or the congregation of a church, he creates disarray, arguments, and splits. This discredits the person and work of Christ.

"There should be such a bond among Christians," says Reese, "that when the world looks at us it should be amazed at the oneness of the body. They should know we are Christians by our love. They should say, 'Wow! Jesus must be God if He can give such love and unity to a diverse group of people.' When the work is divided, we're not exhibiting the fact that Jesus Christ is really God or that the Trinity is One.

"Every page in the Bible is devoted to one of two topics. It's about our relationship with God and our relationship with our neighbors, and our two greatest commands are to love the Lord our God with all our hearts and to love our neighbor as ourselves. From the first page to the last, the Bible is a handbook about the relationships of our lives."

This is a subject deeply embedded in Reese's heart. One day recently, he got off the boat at the marina near his home in Sanibel Island. He saw a man cleaning some fish and spoke to him. Over the next few weeks, Reese saw the man several times. He noticed something so pleasant in the man's words and behavior that he finally said to him, "You must be a Christian."

"I'm sorry it took you so long to notice," the man replied.

"It shouldn't take the world very long to notice we're Christians," Reese later observed. "We should be so radical in our attitude of love toward others, so forgiving, so pleasant and strong and kind that others will pick up on it right away."

> **"It shouldn't take the world very long to notice we're Christians..."**

Humility

The wheel of love spins on the axle of humility, as Jesus demonstrated when He washed His disciples' feet. It was literally a 24-foot lesson! He said to His squabbling followers that evening, "You know that those who are considered rulers of the Gentiles lord it over them, and their great ones exercise authority over them. But it shall not be so among you. But whoever would be great among you must be your servant, and whoever would be first among you must be slave of all. For even the Son of Man came not to be served but to serve, and to give his life as a ransom for many" (Mark 10:42-45).

While none of us is an expert in the humility field, it's important for leaders to view themselves as Paul suggests: "Do not think of yourself more highly than you ought, but rather think of yourself with sober judgment, in accordance with the faith God has distributed" (Romans 12:3).[96]

"God gives us spiritual strengths and weaknesses," Reese says. "There are areas in which I'm strong and areas in which I'm weak. For years I tried to do what I lacked. Now I realize I need to do what I can do, and the Lord will provide someone else to do what I can't. If I can stay focused within my bandwidth and stay on my knees, I think we can accomplish things."

In 2 Corinthians 8:12, the Bible says, "If the willingness is there, the gift is acceptable according to what one has, not according to what one does not have." It's alright to have a narrow band of abilities so long as we're willing to do whatever God assigns us.

"The Lord lets us have weaknesses," explains Reese. "He didn't give me a talent to sing. He doesn't expect me to sing solos, but He wants me to be willing to do what He has called me to do. One of the most comforting things in the world is to realize when I can't do something I can say, 'Lord, You know I can't do this.' Every time I pray that prayer God delivers me."

Several years ago this was put to the test when Reese traveled to Nigeria for the dedication of the local Child Evangelism Fellowship headquarters in the city of Kaduna. He had been to

Africa many times and he knew how much time it takes to earn respect and build trust there. Protocol is an important part of the culture, and leadership is important in the African church. Reese had previously traveled to Kaduna for the groundbreaking of the building, had visited again during the construction process, and was now returning for its dedication.

Arriving at the site, he saw cars pulling up from all directions. People assembled in great excitement. Reese walked into the two-story building and looked at the rooms and halls and lobby. They didn't seem finished. There was mildew on the walls and puddles in the hallways. The building was cluttered and hadn't been cleaned as it should have been. Yet many people had traveled for miles to attend the big event, and a festive sense of excitement was building.

As Reese walked through the building, he felt a sinking feeling in his stomach. He said to himself, "I can't dedicate this building for God. It's not been cared for. It's neglected." He sent word for the leaders who were on the national CEF Board to assemble in a particular room. About a dozen gathered around, and Reese said quietly, "Do you believe I love you?"

He went down the line and asked every one of the men and women, "Do you believe I love you and your country?" Each one replied affirmatively: "Yes, you've been here many times. You've helped us again and again. We know you love us."

"You've asked me to come to dedicate this building to the glory of God and for His honor," Reese said, "and I'm here to tell you I can't do this. This building is a disgrace. We should repent and ask God to forgive us and help us get this job done for His glory and honor."

When the time came for the dedication service, the chairman of the national board stood up and told the crowd, "We came here today to dedicate this building, but we aren't going to do that. We're going to repent of our sins." He explained with sorrow the unprepared and untended state of the building and asked forgiveness. Others did the same. Suddenly the audience stood and applauded. The crowd quickly mobilized, got to work, and within a few days they had a building for which they could all be proud and thankful.

The only reason Reese was able to exert that kind of leadership was because he loved these leaders enough to be confrontational when he had to be. That isn't the opposite of humility, but its essence. Today the building is being used as a center for the work of child evangelism across the African continent and for the glory of God.

"I don't think I could have done that if I'd been a rookie president," says Reese, reflecting on the difficult experience. "I've been the president of CEF now for about a third of the life of the organization, and there is something to be said for building respect and authority over time. If a leader has respect and presence, things change. The Bible says, 'Leaders who know their business and care keep a sharp eye out for the shoddy and cheap' (Proverbs 20:8).[97] When a leader walks into the room, things change. He or she comes in with a presence that should have an influence. It's like a teacher walking into a classroom."

Many businesses and organizations fail—or they don't progress as they should—because their leaders have neglected a handful of essential but necessary tools. The natural abilities God gave Reese and his leadership team, refined in the fires of business and industry, have provided CEF with leadership that fulfills the description of Proverbs 16:15: "Good-tempered leaders invigorate lives; they're like spring rain and sunshine."[98]

Integrity

Another vital tool of leadership is the plumb line of integrity. In studying the history of Christian organizations, Reese noticed a disturbing pattern. Many of them began on a solid theological foundation, with a clear mission and a courageous task. But over time and with successive changes of leadership, many of them drifted away until they no longer resembled the work envisioned by their founders. We can see this in the Ivy League schools and in many denominations and churches. Through a slow process of deterioration, compromise, and change, these organizations accepted leaders with different views. The boards and board members adopted new standards and convictions, and there was a liberalizing of the nature of the organization's work.

"To keep this from happening at Child Evangelism Fellowship," Reese says, "I went around the country constantly pounding home certain issues. As time went by, these issues began to formulate in my heart as 'culture points.' I compiled them into a list that has become known as the CEF Culture Points. Now CEF chapters all over the world have these culture points displayed in their offices, our leaders teach them, and our missionaries follow them."

1. IMPORTANCE OF GODLY LEADERSHIP AT EVERY LEVEL. Spiritual leadership is the highest form of authority. The men and women who lead must have a personal heart for God in order to be able to discern the will of God and lead the ministry effectively. Regardless of the skill of a leader,

if he or she lacks a heart for God, the work will be eroded at its very foundation.

2. IMPORTANCE OF THE SPIRITUAL WELFARE OF OUR WORKERS. It is vital that we are never satisfied to simply teach our staff the methods of how to reach children and how to train others to do so, but we must purposefully invest in the spiritual lives of our staff. When the CEF staff is made up of men and women who are primarily driven by passion for God and His glory and have a clear call from the Lord, the work will prosper. If we keep our focus on God and on His calling, then we will be sustained in times of challenge.

3. IMPORTANCE OF PRAYER AS OUR FOUNDATION. It is not the work we do, the meetings we hold or the decisions we make that bring the greatest advances in the work; it is the time spent before the throne of God in prayer, in the name of our Lord Jesus Christ, that brings power, laborers and resources into the ministry.

4. IMPORTANCE OF EVANGELIZING CHILDREN. There is no limit to the number of organizations that do many good things that are important to boys and girls in need. We are thankful for them and believe that God uses them to help hurting children. CEF, however, has been called by God to make it our highest priority to present the Gospel so children may be saved and discipled in God's Word. We must stay on point.

5. IMPORTANCE OF A CLEAR AND BIBLICAL PRESENTATION OF THE GOSPEL. The fact that a young child can comprehend the simple message of salvation and become a child

of God is the foundational principle of CEF. Everything else that we do is based upon this fact. The Good News of Jesus Christ is the power of God unto salvation. We must present it clearly and accurately.

6. IMPORTANCE OF A COMMITMENT TO EXCELLENCE, FOR THE GLORY OF GOD. Every aspect of the work, no matter how big or small, has significance. This includes the training we conduct, the materials we produce, the facilities we use and the way we present ourselves. In every area we must strive for excellence to the glory of God!

Everyone has leadership skills, and we're all leaders in some form, forum, or fashion. God wants you to wield the leverage of leadership in the groups in which He has placed you—in home, school, business, and church. Learn to use the fulcrum of faith, the pulley of vision, the wheel of love, and the axil of humility. Maintain your integrity. As the apostle Paul said, "In his grace, God has given us different gifts for doing certain things well. So... if God has given you leadership ability, take the responsibility seriously" (Romans 12:6 and 8).[99]

CHAPTER 16

Giving

REESE RECALLS, "I'M PASSIONATE ABOUT THE PRIVILEGE OF GIVING, FOR THAT'S ONE OF THE MOST INDELIBLE LESSONS I LEARNED IN CHILDHOOD. My father pastored a church heavily invested in global missionary outreach. It held the reputation of having the highest levels of giving to missions, per capita, of any church in America. A key element in the program was the church's annual Global Outreach Conference, during which everyone was expected to make a financial pledge to the missionary budget."

Every year of Reese's childhood, he awaited the final night of the conference with excitement. He vividly recalls his uncle, who was an accountant, sitting on the platform near the pulpit with a calculating machine. The cards were turned in one by one, and someone read off each commitment, which was entered into the machine. At the conclusion of the process, Reese's uncle dramatically pulled the lever of the machine for the final total. Every year the goal was met.

"One year when I was in elementary school," says Reese, "I wanted to be included in the excitement. Filling out a commitment card, I pledged to give five dollars over the next 12 months. Since I made 50 cents a week doing chores at home, and since my family took a two-week vacation every year, I knew I could fulfill my pledge by giving a dime a week from my allowance for 50 weeks."

That's what he did. "Every Sunday for the next year, I took a dime to church. Pulling an envelope from the rack on the back of the pew, I filled in the information with a pencil, inserted my dime, licked the envelope, and dropped it in the offering plate. It probably drove the church treasurer crazy, because he had to extract the dime and record the information by hand each week, but it was the best thing in the world for me. I learned early the joy of regular sacrificial missionary giving."

A few years later, Reese's annual missionary pledge occasioned his first debt, as he borrowed money for the first time in his life in order to fulfill his pledge. He was in high school and his best friend was Carter Boyd. The two were walking home from school on the railroad tracks when Reese asked Carter if he could borrow some money from him. He needed $23 to fill his commitment that year. "I think I'd pledged $100," Reese says, "but I was short. He loaned me the money on the condition I give him back the entire amount at once, not in smaller increments, as he didn't want to be tempted to fritter his money away dollar by dollar. I promised to do so, and thus fulfilled my pledge while learning to be responsible with debt. The Lord enabled me to learn early in life to manage my finances from the perspective of giving to the Lord."

It was a habit that returned in blessing. "I still marvel at the way God provided for me in high school," says Reese. "I went to a school that had a lot of rich kids, and my family was poor. Yet somehow as I looked around, I realized I had everything these rich kids had. We lived in a nice house—the parsonage provided by the church—and it was in a nice part of town. The local car dealer gave my dad a new vehicle to drive every year. And as I made and fulfilled my annual missionary pledge, the Lord blessed me with the ability to make money. From age ten, I bought my own clothes. I always had money in my pockets because God blessed me. I had lawns to mow, and I acquired customers easily. I always carried trimmers in my back pocket and could pop into people's yards to keep their lawns serviced. I learned to build up a customer base and follow up on referrals, and in the winter I carried a snow shovel house-to-house and cleaned their sidewalks and driveways.

"I'm convinced the Lord blessed me like this because even as a teenager, by His grace, I was faithful in tithing and in giving to missions. Because my dad was a pastor I knew my local church should be supported, but I also knew there was a great need for financing the missionary enterprise of reaching the nations for Christ."

WHEN I DIDN'T TITHE

For a time early in my career, I got out of the habit of tithing. It was near the end of my time at Best Lock, and the company changed the way I got paid. They moved me from a rather generous salary to straight commission. Well, whenever our patterns of income change we have to deliberately think about readjusting the way we give. I failed to do that. My income moved from being regular to sporadic and I got off rhythm in giving. I lost my confidence when I went out to sell. I was too young to be calling on major corporations, and I became aware of my age, felt insecure, and lost my fire. During that time I taught a Sunday school class for junior high boys. One Sunday morning the lesson was on tithing. Then I was asked to teach a class of senior high students that evening. Since I had a lesson already prepared from the morning, I taught the same lesson. After class I slipped into the back of the church for the evening service. The topic of the pastor's message was also on tithing. I bowed my head and said, "Lord, you have brought this to my mind three times today. I repent. When I get paid again I will be faithful and diligent and will get caught up again on this."

Having prayed that prayer, it's interesting to note that I had not actually given anything to the Lord yet. I had simply determined to do so; yet the Lord honored my intention. As I was getting out of my car at the plant the next morning, someone handed me a pink phone message slip. When I entered the doors, there was another message. In my office was another. They were all customers wanting me to call on them. The orders started coming in so fast that several weeks later the company asked me to take a week of vacation because they couldn't keep up with the work.[100]

Stewardship is taught throughout the Bible, but Reese has been especially impacted by his study of 2 Corinthians 8 and 9, the Bible's premier chapters about giving. Here we learn that giving is not a command but a privilege (2 Corinthians 8:8). It's based on the example of our Lord Jesus Christ, who gave up everything for us (v. 9). Giving is a joint operation of our intentions coupled with our follow-through (v. 11). As a general rule, tithing should be intentional, not just impulsive. While there are times to give spontaneously, our primary stewardship should be planned, methodical, and regular (vv. 12-15). The Lord desires a willing heart and wholehearted devotion.

This passage also promises rich blessings to those who give. "Each one must give as he has decided in his heart," the apostle Paul wrote, "not reluctantly or under compulsion, for God loves a cheerful giver. And God is able to make all grace abound to you, so that having all sufficiency in all things at all times, you may abound in every good work" (2 Corinthians 9:7-8). We shouldn't shy away from the promises God offers to those who give, but we should wisely claim them by faith.

This is a point about which Reese feels strongly. "On one occasion," he recalls, "I was teaching an adult Sunday school class, and we had a teachers' meeting each Wednesday to discuss the lesson for the upcoming Sunday. One week the subject was stewardship, and the leader warned us not to discuss the blessing that comes from giving. This was a subject that had been abused by some television preachers, and the church elders apparently wanted to avoid it altogether."

Reese spoke up and asked, "Where in the Bible is there a giving passage that doesn't discuss the ensuing blessing to givers?"

No answer was given.

"Aren't we to teach the whole counsel of God?" he asked. "We do not give in order to get. But we do give to get to give." He went on to explain, "This is the cycle of sufficiency. This is God's way for us to receive, that we may continue to give abundantly. Your accountant can't explain it. It's a mystery, like prayer. But I keep going back to my high school years. Why is it that although I came from a poor family, I had everything the rich kids had? I always had yards to mow. I always had money in my pocket. I always had all I needed. I believe it was because I learned from childhood the secrets of giving. I once heard a man say that when he counseled young couples in financial difficulty, he told them to increase their giving before doing anything else. It doesn't make sense to a secular financial counselor, but it makes total faith-sense. We give so we will receive so that we'll be able to give some more."

Pastors often call on Reese to speak on the subject of tithing because he does so, not from the perspective of pastoring, but from the viewpoint of a business leader. But he is also quick to point out that giving doesn't just apply to money.

"When I was in business, I began tithing my time to God as well. The principles of 2 Corinthians 8 and 9 apply to all of life. They apply to time. We don't all have the same amount of money, but we do have the same amount of time—24 hours a day, from the richest to the poorest of us. As you give your time to the Lord, He blesses it. You'll accomplish more by being generous with your time than you will if you keep it all to yourself."

During Reese's years at Kauffman Products, he kept careful track of his time. At one point his "tithe" of time reached 60 percent as he was involved in church work, speaking at retreats, and serving on the boards of ministries he believed in. He learned that when one gives time to God, somehow God gives it back in supernatural ways. We'll end up with more time for those things that represent the desires of our hearts. "I have more fun doing things than anyone I know," says Reese. "I have more fun by accident then most people have intentionally. I believe it's because I've learned to give my time to the Lord and He has returned it to me with joy."

Since Reese traces his instincts about giving back to a childhood pledge to missions, he zealously encourages parents to teach their children the joy of giving at an early age. If we teach children to give from the earliest time they have any money at all, it will become a natural habit for them, just as natural as learning to walk. If we teach them from childhood to be cheerful givers because Christ gave Himself to them, it becomes a part of who they are. They will benefit throughout life by being givers.

> **If we teach them from childhood to be cheerful givers because Christ gave Himself to them, it becomes a part of who they are.**

Reese's parents always taught him to tithe from his allowance or any little earnings that came his way, and he grew up hearing testimonies of God's provisions. "My grandfather, who came to the Lord later in life, was a tool and die maker. The week he got saved he took two dollars from his paycheck and gave it to my father, who was a pastor. No one knows where he learned that he needed to tithe, but from the moment of his conversion he started tithing. These family stories impacted me. My dad's example influenced me. My parents' teaching informed me. And my youthful missionary pledge taught me the reality of the joy of giving. No child should miss out on something as rich as that!"

Prayer

NY CHILD WOULD ENJOY REESE'S OFFICE AT THE CHILD EVANGELISM FELLOWSHIP INTERNATIONAL HEADQUARTERS WITH ITS SITTING AREAS, SHIP MODELS, NAUTICAL GEAR, AND INTERESTING PICTURES AND PLAQUES. But only one child has really been at home there—Bucky Kauffman. Growing up, he was always welcome in his dad's office in Warrenton, and he often played on the floor or read in a chair while Reese worked. Reese would pull out the center drawer from his desk and put it on the floor so Bucky could play with the rubber bands, paper clips, magnets, and other items in that horizontal treasure trove. But a few years passed and one day Reese noticed Bucky wasn't coming into the office anymore.

"Bucky, you've not been up to my office for a long time."

"Well, dad, you're always so busy. And besides, they won't let me in."

"Who won't let you in?"

"Your secretaries."

Reese put his hands on the boy's shoulders and told him, "Bucky, whenever you want to come into my office, you don't have to ask anyone. You come in whenever you want. If I can't spend time with you right then I'll tell you, but you can always come into my office whenever you want—anytime."

Nothing happened for about a week. Then one day as Reese conducted an important meeting the door burst open and in came Bucky. Standing behind him in alarm were two secretaries. Reese greeted his son as if he were President of the United States. Bucky settled in for awhile that day, just like old times, and Reese felt good having him there. Bucky was exercising his sonship.

"That's exactly what prayer is," Reese explains. "It's exercising our rights as children of God. We have a standing invitation to enter the throne room whenever we want. When Jesus died on the cross, the veil of the temple was ripped apart, giving us full access into the Holy of Holies. We can come with boldness and with unrestricted utterance. We can say things to God we cannot say to anyone else. He understands our infirmities. We can have an intimacy with Him that we cannot have even with our closest friends, not even with a spouse. God automatically understands us in a way no one else can, even in a way we ourselves cannot understand.

"Furthermore, the One with whom we have this relationship is someone who can do things no one else can do. He is the creator and sustainer of the universe. He can do anything, is all-powerful, and is constantly available to act on our behalf. If we can grasp these truths about prayer, it changes our lives. When we start practicing prayer in a biblical way, it turns our thinking around."

Though Reese grew up knowing how to pray, it was the simple words of evangelist Fred Brown that triggered a set of lifelong habits far beyond anything the old preacher could have imagined: "Tomorrow when you drive to work, take your right hand and turn the knob to the left and spend time talking with God." How remarkable that such a plain sentence could travel so far in one listener's heart!

There are a thousand benefits to prayer beyond simply the answers we receive. We find our attitudes, our thinking, our behavior, and our personalities being changed simply by the practice of continual prayer.

The Difficulty of Prayer

Those who claim prayer is easy are probably not spending much time doing it. Prayer is sometimes difficult, and a Christian who is serious about praying becomes an instant candidate for Satan's hit list. When we purposely try to keep prayer commitments, we find prayer to be arduous. The Bible refers to intercession as laboring, striving, agonizing, and wrestling. It's important to view prayer in those terms because otherwise we might grow discouraged.

"I personally believe that Satan, the adversary, is a diabolical personage who also represents a highly organized force coming against us," Reese teaches. "I believe he opposes the prayer life like no other part of the Christian experience. All the other disciplines of the Christian life can be performed with a cold heart. You can read your Bible with a cold heart. You can give money with a cold heart. You can go to church with a cold heart. Lots of people in church are sitting there with cold hearts. We can do things out of heartless habit. We shouldn't, but we can and do. You cannot get alone with God and truly spend time with Him and have a cold heart. You cannot get alone in a room on your knees by your chair or go on a prayer walk with a cold heart. When you're not right with the Lord you don't want to be in His presence. To be intimate with God, you've got to have a warm heart toward Him."

In motivating people toward a deeper prayer life, Reese has detected a common difficulty. People say to him, "Okay, Reese, I'm going to pray. I've heard you speak on this subject, and I'm going to do it." But the first thing that happens is their minds begin to wander. We often get interrupted when we try to pray. If you're drowning in the ocean or a bear is charging at you, you'll pray. But what about sustained daily fellowship that requires purity of heart and intimacy with God?

"Sometimes I try to pray and it seems like my words are hitting an iron ceiling," Reese admits, "but the important thing is not how I feel about my prayers but whether or not I am truly praying. Since prayer is difficult, there are times when it's really hard to pray because it's such a battle. Other times it's not a battle. Sometimes it's like driving a car with the top down. You feel ready access to Heaven. There were times when I drove up to my plant ready to pull into the parking lot, but I was having such a wonderful time with the Lord I just drove around the block because I didn't want it to end. Sometimes it's easy and sometimes it difficult, but God hears prayer regardless."

When he teaches about prayer, Reese approaches it from several perspectives—how we prepare to pray; the value of our prayers; the motivation, location, and organization of our prayer lives; the vital role of prayer partners; and the overwhelming mystery of God, who invites us to pray and responds when we do so. Quality time in prayer begins, Reese believes, with preparation for prayer.

Preparation for Prayer

Reese often mentions the warning of Psalm 66:18, that if we regard iniquity in our hearts, the Lord will not hear us. We cannot allow sins, either open or secret ones, to clog the lines. Having a good talk with the Lord involves honesty and confession. Isaiah 59:1-2 says, "Behold, the Lord's hand is not shortened, that it cannot save, or his ear dull, that it cannot hear; but your iniquities have made a separation between you and your God, and your sins have hidden his face from you." In approaching His presence, we must be sensitive to anything that would hinder our prayers and confess our faults and failures quickly and earnestly with a desire for His cleansing and overcoming grace.

The Value of Prayer

We also need to appreciate the value of prayer, says Reese. There's both an objective and subjective value to prayer. The objective value is the answer we receive. We may be praying for things all over the world, and God answers. We have tangible results that become items of praise and thanksgiving. But there are subjective benefits to prayer too. When we pray, we're enjoying the presence and fear of God, and that has all kinds of value for us.

"When driving to my home on Sanibel Island in Florida," Reese says, "I have to cross a causeway that is three miles long; it's a long and narrow bridge. There is often bumper to bumper traffic. From time to time someone will get out of the line, pass several cars, and then try to cut back in. That always irritates me. If I were alone in the car, I might express my frustration. But suppose I had the Lord Jesus sitting on the passenger side? That would change my way of responding. I might say, 'Well, the dear man must have an emergency, he must be in a hurry.'"

Or take the effect prayer has on fear. There have been times when Reese recalls walking around the grounds of CEF Headquarters late at night completely overwhelmed by the financial needs of the ministry. It sat on his shoulders like stacked-up anvils. But then he learned to ask himself, "Would I be afraid of anything if the Lord Jesus Christ were standing physically at my side?" That radically changes the picture. Prayer is the visualization and realization of the presence of Christ between our fears and us. When we practice the privilege of prayer, we are practicing the presence of God. It's an atmosphere that seeps into our spirits and reshapes our responses in life. The value is inestimable.

The Motivation for Prayer

That brings us to why we pray. There are many reasons, of course. We pray because we're commanded to pray; it's a matter of simple obedience. We pray because of its objective benefits—the answers we receive. We're also motivated when we realize its subjective benefits—the improvements that come into our souls and spirits. But none of these represent the greatest motivation. Reese teaches that we should want to pray simply because we love the Lord, for when two people are in love they want to be together.

"I often ask an audience if anyone present is engaged to be married," Reese says. "If so, we expect them to act a little strange. They're flushed with love. When my daughter Michelle came home from college to wait for her fiancé, Mitch, to graduate, she wanted to talk to him all the time. In those days the long-distance phone rates dropped at 11:00 at night. What do you think happened at our house at 11:01 every night? The phone came alive. Sometimes as I walked through the house, I'd hear her end of the conversation. They talked about the most inconsequential things. 'What did you have for lunch today, sweetheart?' They just wanted to hear each other's voice because of the freshness of their love for the other. That's why we pray."

STRANGE IMPRESSIONS

Once when I finished a talk in Belgium, a woman with a weathered face came up to me. Her name was Esther; her head was wrapped in a scarf. "Mr. Kauffman," she said, "will you pray for the children of Belgium?" We were in a hurry and our leaders were trying to get me away, but her face made an impression on me. I knew the international children in Belgium were coming to know the Lord, but the indigenous Belgian children were not. "Will you pray for them?" she said. The scarf-wrapped face of that woman has stayed with me, and I've prayed for years for the children of Belgium.

On another trip a lady in Kenya named Josephine asked me to pray for her four children, who were getting into trouble. Her request impressed my heart. I've never seen her again, and I'm not sure when to stop praying for her and her children. That was years ago, but I still pray for her and those four children every day.

The greatest gift you can give to others is to pray for them.

The Location of Prayer

Where do we pray? Everyone's life is built around certain routines that develop over the years. In one sense, we learn to pray continuously. As Reese discovered in the front seat of his car when he turned the radio dial to the left, Jesus is with us wherever we are. "I've learned to give my waiting time to God," he says. "If I'm waiting for an airplane, in the doctor's office, or on the phone on hold, I've learned to convert that time from wasted time to prayer time."

> **"I've learned to give my waiting time to God...I've learned to convert that time from wasted time to prayer time."**

Prayer is the greatest communication system ever invented because it works anytime, anywhere. It never runs out of power. It always has a clear signal. Its batteries never die, and you always have a full set of bars. You can pray silently, aloud, extendedly, or briefly. God always leans over to listen.

Yet the Bible does talk about having a prayer closet (Matthew 6:6). We need a habitual, daily place and time for regular prayer. It might be a trail in the woods or a desk in the basement. We're blessed when we have a place where we meet God by routine appointment. These times become sacred to us.

"Once in my travels I stayed in someone's home and was given the bedroom of the teenage son," says Reese. "I noticed he had a closet with a sliding door. All his shirts were on one side and the longer items were on the other. Down on the floor were a Bible, a notebook, and a flashlight. This young man—a spiritual giant in the making—literally went into his closet and prayed as Jesus commanded.

"A friend of mine lived with four children in a small house. He took me to his garage, which housed a furnace, water heater, and miscellaneous equipment. He had nailed up some plywood and made a small room with a door. It was about the size of a phone booth. There he had a little chair, light, and shelf for his Bible and prayer lists.

"There is no excuse for not having a personal prayer closet of some sort. It might be a favorite chair or the front seat of your car or a small desk in the spare bedroom. But each of us needs a sanctified place. What does it do to a wife to see her husband developing that kind of habit? What does it mean to a pastor to know his people are praying like that? How do you think a dad or mom feels knowing their son or daughter is meeting with the Lord each day in a sacred place of prayer? It brings a peace, joy, and security that nothing else can give."

A habit is something we do so often it becomes involuntary. It becomes natural. We have habits about how we comb our hair, how we get dressed, how we put on our socks. We don't think about it. Prayer should be the same. Yes, there is spontaneous prayer, but we should also build patterns into our daily schedules to remind us to pray. The great men and women of God through history differ in their gifts and personalities, but they have one thing in common—they are great in prayer. Some were scholars, others were not; all were gifted in one way or another. But the one thing true of them all—they knew to pray.

The Organization of Prayer

Prayer should have some organization to it. Have you noticed the importance of being organized? Isn't everything in the Christian life organized? When we go to church there's an agenda for the service. When we read the Bible each day, it doesn't just flip itself open; we have some system. If we only pray when there's a crisis or when we happen to think about it, that's unhealthy. Reese advocates committed prayer and prayer commitments.

"The Christian life requires commitments," he says, "those we make to other people and to God. We should pray for our loved ones every day, for family members, for church leaders. We want them to remain strong. While we can't pray about everything everyday, some things are worthy of a daily prayer commitment. When you make a commitment to prayer, it must be so strong you cannot break it. You've got to become radical. My personal rule is: I don't put my head on my pillow at night until I've covered all my prayer commitments. If I say, 'The Lord knows I'm tired today, I've been traveling, I'll catch up later,' well, within three months my commitments would have fallen through and my prayer life would be in ruins.

> **When you make a commitment to prayer, it must be so strong you cannot break it.**

"Once when I was speaking at Cedarville University about the importance of prayer commitments, I told the students, 'If anyone would like me to make up a personal prayer plan for you, I'd be happy to do it.' I got over 1,700 requests! I made a plan for each one of them. It was a job! But I helped them categorize their prayers. One section was for family, one for their studies or vocation or business. I would suggest four or five categories, and even up to ten or twelve. We made up a three-ring notebook for each student, using three-by-five cards, with dividers and tabs marking the categories. All this could be done electronically today, of course, but this was before the digital age.

"Some divisions were for daily prayer. Some were for praying on Mondays, Tuesdays, and so forth. We divided their prayer plans into seven groups, distributing the load over seven days so beginners could handle it. When the students went into the day, they had a card for Monday, or whatever day it was. By the end of the week, they had covered all their prayer needs and commitments. This is the way I start everyone off. I've prepared these cards and notebooks for thousands of people over the decades.

"My own personal prayer life has developed beyond the card system. Now I just need key words that serve as 'triggers.' In my pocket right now is a folded sheet of paper with the categories I've committed to pray about on a daily basis. I could tell you this list verbatim, but I still find the list helpful to hold in my hand. As I go through the day I work my way through it. The apostle Paul told people that he made mention of them always in his prayers, and I want to follow his example."

If you get a glimpse of Reese's prayer list, you'll notice it has five columns. In the first column he has a list of words that indicate his own personal spiritual needs. He feels the most important person we pray about every day is ourselves. It's not selfish to ask God to work within oneself what is pleasing to Him. We need to pray about our own spiritual needs. This includes a time of confession of sin and a request specifically asking the

Holy Spirit for help. We can ask the Spirit to help us in the area of pride and humility. Pride can ruin people. It's a terrible task-master. The only way we can recognize pride, which comes in so many forms, is within the prayer closet as the Lord inspects our hearts and we confess our sins.

"I have another trigger word in this column that reminds me to pray to seek first God's Kingdom and His glory," says Reese. "Another trigger reminds me to pray for the love of Christ—for the kindness, gentleness, and patience He wants me to exhibit. I also ask God to help me see His hand in the circumstances of the day, to help me look for anything He is doing around me. If I can see that, it strengthens my day. I pray for a love of the Word of God, for wisdom, understanding, and discernment. I ask God to help me develop a grateful heart, as I'm happiest when I'm grateful. I pray for love toward my family and staff. It's much easier to live and work with people we love.

> **"...I have another area that has
> been helpful to me—I pray for
> the danger zones of life."**

"Then I have another area that has been helpful to me—I pray for the danger zones of life. These hazardous areas come in all forms. The zones may not be bad in themselves, but I have to be careful. Suppose I don't feel good; I may be tired and jet-lagged—that's a danger zone. I can make mistakes that can't easily be retracted or that can hurt other people. I ask God for grace to help with any danger zone I traverse during the day. I also pray I'll not be judgmental or critical, even in what I think in my heart. I don't want to have critical thoughts, even if I don't express them.

"Then I ask God to empower the gifts He's given me. I need the empowerment of the Holy Spirit for accomplishing things far beyond understanding and ability. Remember the lessons of Luke 11 and Luke 18, where the widow and the midnight neighbor make known their requests with such persistence they cannot be denied. We have to be radical about persevering in prayer.

"Another trigger word on this list is 'godliness.' It's important to pray, 'Lord, I do not want any ungodly areas in my life. I want everything influenced by You.'

"My last trigger in that column is God's will. If you do anything in your life that isn't in God's will, you're wasting your time."

The second column on Reese's prayer paper is family. Here he has the names of his loved ones. The third column consists of colleagues at Child Evangelism Fellowship, including the entire senior staff, plus special friends and ministry partners of CEF.

The fourth column is devoted to the ministries of CEF and its regional directors.

His fifth and final column is a combination of people and things: overseas works, other ministries, prodigals and their parents, and so forth. This is where Reese puts those miscellaneous requests that arise from souls and situations he encounters.

"All through the day I'm working my way through those columns," Reese says. "And yet I'll have to say my best times in prayer come after I've prayed through my commitments and I can talk to the Lord about whatever comes to mind. Prayer, after all, is enjoying the presence of our Heavenly Father."

The Partnership of Prayer

Reese is also a zealous advocate of recruiting a small handful of serious prayer partners. This custom began one day when a man named Larry Green phoned him. Reese didn't know him; yet this man asked if Reese and Linda would join him and his wife on a vacation to the Bahamas. The Greens were looking for a Christian couple to be with. Reese met Larry for lunch, and subsequently the two couples went off on their trip. Night after night, Larry and Reese sat out by the water and talked. They started sharing prayer requests, often about their mutual business concerns or their children and their needs. Returning to Indianapolis, they kept meeting for prayer.

Prayer partners become a tremendous source of exhortation, encouragement, and protection.

"A prayer partner gets to know you so well that he or she can sometimes just look at you and know how to pray," Reese says. "You develop a relationship that goes beyond normal acquaintance. Larry and I talk frequently and pray for each other daily. We now live in different parts of the country, but we purposely get together several times a year—we sit and talk about the Lord. Our families even vacation together. Prayer partners become a tremendous source of exhortation, encouragement, and protection.

"Many Christians miss a great blessing by not cultivating prayer partners. The beauty of a long-term relationship in prayer is looking back over the years to see what God has done."

"HELP LARRY REALIZE HOW LITTLE HE'S GOT TO DO WITH IT"

Years ago when we lived in Indianapolis, I met with two or three other men every Wednesday night. One night, Larry Green didn't show up. We knew he was at church, but he never joined us in our prayer room. Later we saw him in the lobby. He came up to us and simply said, "Do you know what Francis Hansen prayed? He prayed, 'Lord, help Larry realize how little he's got to do with it anyhow.'"

Larry explained he was on his way to meet us when he ran into Francis Hansen, an employee for the state of Indiana. Larry didn't want to be detained by Francis, because he was greatly burdened about some problems he was facing that weekend and wanted to pray with us. But he was pulled aside by this state employee, who said to him, "Larry, is there anything I can pray about?"

Larry didn't think Francis would understand the burdens of his business, but he told him a little about them and Francis prayed for him. His prayer was, "Lord, help Larry realize how little he's got to do with it anyhow."

Those words deeply impressed Larry, and they impressed the rest of us in an unusual way. It's since become a famous prayer in our circle. We're often overwhelmed with problems, like we're bearing the weight of the world. We think everything depends on us, but God diverted Larry that night to teach us a lesson. We have so little to do with things because God controls it all.

–Reese Kauffman

The Mystery of Prayer

God is a God of intelligence, and everything about Him is rational, yet we also know He's an infinite God and everything about Him is mysterious. Prayer is logical, but it's also deeply mysterious. "For example," Reese says, "I've never fully comprehended why Jesus told the disciples, 'The harvest is plentiful, but the laborers are few. Therefore pray earnestly to the Lord of the harvest to send out laborers into His harvest.' Jesus spoke those words to the 72 workers He was sending out. He told them to pray for more workers. Well, why didn't Jesus just send out 720 to begin with? Or 72,000? Why did He send out only 72, and then tell them to pray for more? To me that's an unanswerable question. Why would God send out fewer workers than needed, telling the ones He is sending to pray for more?"

There's a mystery in prayer woven into the omniscient inscrutability of the Almighty. Somehow our prayers move an omnipotent God to do things He might not otherwise do. We don't understand that, but it puts a frame around the awesome responsibility and power of prayer.

> **There's a mystery in prayer woven into the omniscient inscrutability of the Almighty. Somehow our prayers move an omnipotent God to do things He might not otherwise do.**

"At the moment Jesus died on the cross," Reese teaches, "the veil in the temple was torn from top to bottom. This was the 23-foot-high veil separating the Holy Place from the Holy of Holies in the Temple. It barred the presence of God from everyone except the High Priest. Suddenly the barrier was torn away.

Hebrews 10 says, 'Therefore, brothers, since we have confidence to enter the holy places by the blood of Jesus, by a new and living way that he opened for us through the curtain, that is, through his flesh... let us draw near with a true heart in full assurance of faith' (vv. 19-22). We're to come boldly and with confidence to the throne of grace to find mercy there and grace to help in times of need (Hebrews 4:16). We're to come and exercise our rights as children of God."

Sometimes people ask Reese, "Aren't you a little radical about prayer?"

"Yeah," he admits, "I think I am. But if we're going to be radical about something, don't you think it ought to be prayer?"

CHAPTER 18
Enthusiasm

O NE DAY WHEN REESE WAS IN BUSINESS, HE ARRIVED AT HIS OFFICES AT KAUFFMAN PRODUCTS, INC. in Indianapolis just as the phone rang. A plane had crashed into White River just behind the hospital and the police wanted to know if Reese, a trained rescue diver, could help with the rescue or recovery effort. Reese raced to the scene, his tags and credentials getting him through police barricades and checkpoints. Opening the trunk of his car, he began donning scuba gear and coordinating with other members of his diving team, who were also putting on their wetsuits and tanks.

Reese and two partners went into the water. They were searching for the small plane, which had been underwater for about an hour and a half. There was no visibility in the river. It was muddy, and the divers could only grope and feel their way in the black water. As a cave diver Reese was used to that, but it was different knowing someone was trapped and almost certainly drowned.

Finally, they found the plane. They didn't know how many bodies it held, and with zero visibility it was difficult to know how to proceed. They could only feel their way with their hands. The divers tied grappling lines to various parts of the plane so it could be hauled out of the water; but every time the crane tried to lift the vehicle, parts of the plane broke off. Reese informed his fellow divers that he thought he could find the door to the plane and would try to open it and pull the rope through the cockpit so they could secure a line around the fuselage.

"Still working without visibility," Reese remembers, "I opened the door and swam through the cockpit, knowing I was swimming over the bodies of the victims. Suddenly a hand reached through the mud and grabbed my wrist and squeezed it. It was ghastly, like something from a nightmare. I screamed involuntarily and raced to the surface, my heart beating like a drum."

"Someone is alive," Reese shouted, "but it can't be!"

Another diver surfaced beside him, looked over, and with equal alarm shouted, "Was that you?" He had been swimming through the plane from the opposite direction and had grabbed Reese's hand in the blackness. They nearly scared the daylights out of each other.

The crew eventually got the plane up. The pilot was in the cockpit dead; the passenger had been thrown out but did not survive. The divers found Bibles floating to the surface of the river. It had been a chaplain and his assistant. They recovered the bodies, but Reese will never forget the hand clutching him in the muddy waters like the grip of death.

Reese can tell stories like that all day because he has dabbled in just about everything one can try as a sportsman, including skydiving, cave diving, deep sea diving, swimming, boating, marksmanship, hunting, fishing, off-roading, cross-country motorcycling, skiing on both water and snow—all in addition to being a global traveler, manufacturer, community leader, public speaker, and ministry executive. He advocates plunging into each day with an attitude of adventure, for Jesus promised us life more abundant.

He advocates plunging into each day with an attitude of adventure, for Jesus promised us life more abundant.

God infused Reese with outsized enthusiasm and blessed him with a broad panorama of life experiences. If he has a motto in life, it's "Work hard, play hard." He has done about everything one can do in life. When he's in Colorado, his hobby is driving four-wheelers through the highest passes of the Rockies, exploring old mining roads and ghost towns and taking in vistas seldom seen by busy tourists. He knows most of the trails by heart; he has ridden thousands of miles looking for old roads that haven't been explored since the gold rush days of the old West.

When he's at home in Florida, he does the same with his boats on the bays and open waters of the Gulf of Mexico. He enjoys exploring rivers and bays and little inlets tucked into hidden shorelines.

"I got my love for adventure from my mom, a woman so full of life that she went parasailing only months before her death at age 93," says Reese. "When I was young, whenever we went to an amusement park she'd be the first on the roller coasters. She once hired a hot air balloonist to take her aloft so she'd know what it was like to sail through the sky in a little basket thousands of feet above the ground. She had absolutely no fear. She wanted to tackle the toughest trails when off-roading, even in her ninth decade of life. She'd try anything once. She loved to travel—the further away and more exotic the better. She didn't want to miss the experiences of life."

Reese's love for the water comes from his dad. As Reese grew up, Rev. Kauffman was constantly pointing out streams and rivers and ponds. He wasn't much of a fisherman, but he would always say, "Look at that water over there. Isn't it beautiful? Isn't it good that God let us live close to the river?" Growing up in Indianapolis didn't afford many opportunities for enjoying the beach, but whenever the Kauffmans visited grandparents, they'd be near the Atlantic Ocean.

"It was almost magical to us," says Reese. "I've always been mesmerized by rivers and seas, and I've had boats all my life. For 23 years I boated the river systems of the Ohio, the Kentucky, and the Tennessee Rivers. I know those routes well. The Ohio River is a thousand miles long and has a series of locks—a series of lakes really—and it's very navigable. For our honeymoon, Linda and I took a 1,261-mile trip down the Ohio River and up the Mississippi. The rivers are fun, but it's the oceans that overwhelm me with their vastness, depth, and ever-changing conditions and colors."

Reese got into scuba diving early and was certified as an open water diver and as a cave diver. This is what provided the aforementioned opportunity to work several years with the Indianapolis Police Department on its search-and-rescue team. For a brief time he thought he might enjoy jumping out of airplanes. But when he went out on his first jump, he hit a tree and broke his nose. It was a static-line jump with a T-10 parachute like the military uses, which means the skydiver hits pretty hard. When he saw he was falling right into a tree, he went into tree crash position, fell through the branches, and landed with a thud on the ground. Nothing was hurt except his nose, but he shuddered when he saw a spike sticking up in the ground near the base of the tree and realized how close he had come to "nailing" the jump—literally. He went ahead and jumped the next week, then the next. That was enough for him, but he still cherishes the exhilaration of the experience.

In a similar way, Reese finds it thrilling to be astride a powerful motorcycle. One of the greatest trips of his life was after his son Bucky's graduation from college. After a year of planning, he ordered two BMW 1200 GS motorcycles and customized them for the trip. When the folks at BMW heard what they were doing, they offered to put them through performance riding school free of charge.

With helmet-to-helmet communication and full armored gear, Reese and Bucky started in Key West, Florida, and trekked clear across the nation, across Canada, across Alaska along the famous pipeline, and all the way to the Arctic Ocean. Along the way, they encountered people who seemed amazed that a father and his son would spend a summer together like this. On the way back they rode a ferry into Bellingham, Washington, and a family came up to them. The man said, "I've been watching you guys. Can you give me some counsel? When my son gets to be the age of your son, I'd like to have this kind of relationship with him." It gave Reese a golden opportunity to witness—not only for the Lord but also on behalf of building a close relationship with our children.

"Having fun—the right fun at the right time in the right way for the right reason—is good; it's a godly thing," Reese teaches.

"It's a ministry. I've found that sports and outdoor pursuits give me great opportunities to mentor others—not only my kids but lots of other guys, including members of our Child Evangelism Fellowship staff. When I take our leadership team aboard my boat, for example, and we get away deep into the Gulf of Mexico, far from noise and distractions, we bond and pray and dream. Sometimes it almost feels like it must have felt when the disciples sailed across the Sea of Galilee. You can often sense the Lord's presence in a special way, especially if the weather gets rough!"

Reese likes to gather his leaders or a special group of friends or colleagues to ride trails, build campfires, have adventures, travel to unusual places, or explore the mountains or oceans. It provides unique opportunities to get men into a place where they'll talk about spiritual things. For over 20 years he's gone to Alaska on hunting and fishing trips with a group of close friends and their sons. Sometimes they're dropped by a helicopter or by bush pilots into remote areas where they hunt, fish, fend for themselves, talk about the Lord, pray, and build memories. Once Reese was trapped by a grizzly bear, while his gun was across the way in the hands of the only two fellows in the group who were clueless about how to use it. "That was a faith-building experience for all of us!" Reese recalls.

"I didn't excel in team sports as a child, but we don't have to be sports stars to have fun. Nor do we need lots of money. We just need to make up our minds to enjoy life wherever we are and whenever we can and to cultivate a healthy attitude of adventure. I believe in 'Work hard, play hard' because life requires intensity. Being a spectator doesn't cut it. We need to be participants.

The Bible says God has given us all things richly to enjoy. The kind of fun and play I advocate isn't separated from our spiritual lives but is woven into them like bright threads. I believe God wants us to live abundantly, to rejoice in Him, and to enjoy the eye-popping beauties of the creation He has placed around us. He wants us to praise Him for the glory of His handiwork."

I believe in 'Work hard, play hard' because life requires intensity.

Reese is quick to point out that neither working hard nor playing hard, by themselves, are the greatest things in life. Both work and play are part of a larger scheme. The most exciting thing is trying to bring more people to the Lord and more children to Christ. Every fiber of his being is seeking to open new doors for the ministry of Child Evangelism Fellowship. The greatest thing is reaching every child, even nation, every day—for the glory of Christ. Someone said that living enthusiastically is like having two right hands. When they're the hands of Christ reaching the world through us, how can we not be zealous? The fire of the Spirit burns within us, and His enthusiasm makes the difference.

Before the Storm Breaks

EVERAL YEARS AGO WHILE TRAVELING IN AFRICA, REESE LISTENED TO A STORY BY CEF REGIONAL DIRECTOR RICHARD ACQUAYE, A NIGERIAN WHO NOW LIVES IN GHANA. Richard told about a small African village that built a school on the edge of a cliff. They were very proud of their school. The children played outside the building before and after classes, but from time to time a child would fall off the cliff. When this happened, the victim, often with broken bones or other serious injuries would be rushed on a stretcher to the next town. This caused understandable distress in the village, and much thought went into a solution. What was needed was a clinic, it was said. Every village needs a clinic, especially when children fall off a cliff. The villagers enthusiastically embraced the vision of building a clinic at the base of the cliff so children could get immediate care.

But a few people argued that although a clinic would be wonderful, the real answer was building a fence along the top of the cliff to keep the children from falling to begin with. That didn't seem as exciting to most of the villagers, because fences don't have the same appeal as clinics. There's a glamor to building clinics, and it's easy to motivate people to raise the funds and do the work. Fences don't have the same allure, but preventative measures are paramount.

The truth of this illustration has a strong appeal for everyone at Child Evangelism Fellowship. As Christians we're understandably eager to build clinics at the bottom of the cliff, but we must not neglect the fence at the top. We praise God for rescue missions, drug treatment programs, crisis pregnancy centers, and all the other clinics that Christians have established. All are good and necessary; they reflect the compassion of Christ. We're grateful for all the Christ-based humanitarian works occurring around the world. Yet these programs are designed to solve problems that might be prevented by leading kids to Christ at the beginning of their lives and giving them a strong foundation in God's Word.

Child Evangelism Fellowship is in the business of building fences at the tops of the cliffs where the children are. That's our specific mission. Whenever CEF shares the message of Jesus Christ, it's like building a fence. The power of the cross is the greatest safeguard the world has ever known. It provides guardrails for the most vulnerable among us and guidelines for the most receptive audience in the world.

You can be a vital part of the work.

And there is no greater work. Children have their lives in front of them, and it isn't the Father's will that any of them perish. The Lord can use us to forever change the life of a boy or girl for whom Christ died. He can use you and me to build a fence at the top of the cliff. Perhaps He'll give you an opportunity to win a child to Him today.

How vital to build the fence before it's too late, before the storm breaks.

On Friday, May 2, 2008, the skies over Myanmar darkened with ominous thunderclouds, swirling and billowing like a boiling kettle upside down. A torrential storm lashed the Burmese basin with the most violent weather patterns in its recorded history. Cyclone Nargis obliterated entire towns and villages. More than 138,000 people perished and over 55,000 were reported missing. Those figures are likely low, for experts believe the Burmese government simply stopped counting its dead.

Lost in the statistics is a story the newspapers didn't report. Sometime prior to Cyclone Nargis, a godly woman near Yangon had become deeply burdened for the children of her village. She longed to share Christ with them but didn't know how. Learning that an organization called Child Evangelism Fellowship was offering classes nearby, she traveled 20 miles to sit under the training of a CEF missionary named Renee. Along with 53 other trainees, she learned how to tell Bible stories, how to present the Gospel, and how to establish and conduct CEF Good News Clubs.

Back in her village, she invited local children to her Good News Club and was thrilled when 50 showed up. Over a period of two months, she taught them the Bible, using resources she'd been given. She told the children about the death and resurrection of the Lord Jesus, and she explained the grace of God and carefully told them how to become Christians. One by one she personally led each of those 50 children to faith in Christ. Every single child prayed to receive Jesus as Lord and Savior.

It was while the woman was away on a trip that Cyclone Nargis bore down upon her village. The devastation was complete and the community annihilated, and among the causalities were the 50 children she had led to Christ.

Returning to the scene of the disaster, this woman collapsed in inconsolable tears. But her CEF trainer, Renee, was able to comfort her with the reminder that those 50 little souls were in Heaven now because of her willingness to share God's message. They were with the Lord, alive, walking and talking with the Savior, exploring their heavenly dwellings, beyond the reach of suffering and sorrow. This woman had reached them in time. She had helped them find the hope of Jesus before the storm broke.

May God give us the burden and the blessing of doing the same. As Reese Kauffman said earlier in this book:

Child Evangelism Fellowship has more open doors than ever. The times are urgent and the work is vital. We have a goal of being in every nation on Earth. We long to reach 100 million children each year with the Gospel of Christ. We're grateful for our heritage but even more excited about our future. We've been assigned a great work; and we could do so much more if we had one more person— just one more—helping us reach Every Child, Every Nation, Every Day.

That person is you.

Endnotes

[1] King James Version

[2] Charles Haddon Surgeon, Susannah Spurgeon, and Joseph Harrald, *The Autography of Charles H. Spurgeon, Compiled from his Diary, Volume 1*, (Chicago: Fleming H. Revell Company, 1898), 106.

[3] *Christian History Magazine*, Issue 29 (Volume X, Number 1), p. 2.

[4] According to Wikipedia's entry on world population, there are now 7 billion people on earth, and approximately 26.3 percent of them are under the age of 15.

[5] Source unknown.

[6] http://churchm.ag/porn-stats/

[7] http://www.cdc.gov/violenceprevention/pdf/schoolviolence_factsheet-a.pdf.

[8] http://nces.ed.gov/pubs2011/2011002.pdf

[9] See, for example, Theodore AD, Chang JJ, Runyan DK, Hunter WM, Bangdewala SI, Agans R. *Epidemiologic features of the physical and sexual maltreatment of children in the Carolinas*. Pediatrics 2005; 115: e331-e337. Also Finkelhor D, Ormrod H, Turner H, Hamby S. *The victimization of children and youth: a comprehensive national survey*. Child Maltreatment 2005; 10: 5-25. And Finkelhor D, Jones L, Shattuck A. *Updated Trends in Child Maltreatment*, 2010. Durham, NH. Crimes against Children Research Center, 2011. Available from www.unh.edu/ccrc/pdf/CV203_Updated%20 trends%202010%20FINAL_12-19-11.pdf.

[10] http://www.childhelp.org/pages/statistics

[11] http://www.childhelp.org/pages/statistics

[12] See, for example, "Gaza's Kids Affected Psychologically, Physically by Lifetime of Violence," by Hashem Said, July 31, 2014, at http://america.aljazeera.com/articles/2014/8/1/health-gaza-children.html.

[13] "UN Report Condemns Torture, Sexual Abuse of Syrian Children," by Renee Lewis, February 5, 2014, at http://america.aljazeera.com/articles/2014/2/5/un-report-condemnsunspeakableatrocitiesagainstsyrianchildren.html.

[14] http://www.un.org/en/globalissues/briefingpapers/refugees/.

[15] Gozdziak, Elzbieta M. and Mica N. Bump. *Data and Research on Human Trafficking: Bibliography of Research Based Literature*. Institute for the Study of International Migration. Georgetown University; Washington, DC. Sept. 2008. Pg. 13.

[16] U.S. Department of State, *Trafficking in Persons Report*, June 2008. Pg. 7.

[17] *Commercial Sexual Exploitation Position Statement, UNICEF UK*. (January 28, 2004).

[18] http://www.unicef.org/indonesia/Factsheet_CSEC_trafficking_Indonesia.pdf

[19] https://cafo.org/ovc/statistics/ Of these, 17.9 million have lost both parents.

[20] http://www.globalissues.org/article/26/poverty-facts-and-stats#src4

[21] www.savethechildren.org, in their booklet, "A Life Free from Hunger." The statistics are drawn from R. E. Black, L. H. Allen, Z. A. Bhutta, et al (2008), "Maternal and Child Undernutrition: Global and Regional Exposures and Health Consequences," *The Lancet*, 2008, Jan 19, 371 (9608), 243-60.

[22] www.savethechildren.org , in their booklet, "A Life Free from Hunger." The statistics are drawn from M. de Onis, M. Blossne, and E. Borghi (2011), "Prevalence of Stunting Among Pre-School Children 1990-2020," Growth Assessment and Surveillance Unit, *Public Health Nutrition, 2011*, July 14:1-7.

[23]Anna Warner, 1860.

[24]C. Herbert Woolstone, from his children's hymn, "Jesus Loves the Little Children."

[25]J. B. Phillips New Testament

[26]From a CEF document, "Teaching Children Effectively Level 1," Children's Ministry Institute, 1984/2010.

[27]Luis Bush, *The 4/14 Window* (Colorado Springs: Compassion International 2009), x.

[28]Luis Bush, *The 4/14 Window* (Colorado Springs: Compassion International 2009), x.

[29]New International Version

[30]The Living Bible

[31]George Barna, *Transforming Children into Spiritual Champions* (Ventura, CA: Regal, 2003), 18.

[32]George Barna, *Transforming Children into Spiritual Champions* (Ventura, CA: Regal, 2003), 34, 47.

[33]George Barna, *Transforming Children into Spiritual Champions* (Ventura, CA: Regal, 2003), 42, 46.

[34]J. Irvin Overholtzer, *A Modern Weeping Prophet* (Palisades, CA: International Child Evangelism Fellowship, Inc., 1947/1953), 9.

[35]Norman Rohrer, *The Indomitable Mr. O* (Warrenton, MO: Child Evangelism Fellowship Press, 1970), 44.

[36]From a document in the CEF archives entitled "Historical and Biographical Record of Los Angeles and Vicinity," in a file labeled "Mr. O's Inter off. Correspondence.

[37]Ruth Overholtzer, *From Then Till Now* (Warrenton, MO: Child Evangelism Fellowship Press, 1990), 75.

[38]J. Irvin Overholtzer, *A Modern Weeping Prophet* (Palisades, CA: International Child Evangelism Fellowship, Inc., 1947/1953), 33.

[39]"The Growing Enthusiasm for Child Evangelism" by J. Irvine Overholtzer in *The Sunday School Times*, December 3, 1938, p. 880.

[40]Ruth Overholtzer, *From Then Till Now* (Warrenton, MO: Child Evangelism Fellowship Press, 1990), 82.

[41]J. Irvine Overholtzer, *Open-Air Evangelism* (Pacific Palisades, CA: International Child Evangelism Fellowship, Inc., 1942), 5-6.

[42]J. Irvin Overholtzer, *A Modern Weeping Prophet* (Palisades, CA: International Child Evangelism Fellowship, Inc., 1947/1953), 66.

[43]J. Irvin Overholtzer, *A Modern Weeping Prophet* (Palisades, CA: International Child Evangelism Fellowship, Inc., 1947/1953), 70.

[44]From a document entitled "Some Personal Observations Regarding Mr. Overholtzer" in the CEF archives in a folder titled "Testimonies and Personal Observations Pertaining to Mr. Overholtzer.

[45]J. Irvin Overholtzer, *A Modern Weeping Prophet* (Palisades, CA: International Child Evangelism Fellowship, Inc., 1947/1953), 69.

[46]Letter from Cutler B. Whitwell of the Fuller Evangelist Foundation, dated April 22, 1946, in the CEF archives.

[47]Interview with J. Edwin Orr, April 12, 1967, transcribed in the file labeled "Testimonies About Mr. O" in the CEF archives. Also see a memo from Mrs. Ruth Overholtzer, dated April 3, 1967, where she writes about Orr: "He is the man who suggested the name for the organization." In CEF archives in folder labeled "Mr. O Book Research."

[48]J. Irvin Overholtzer, *A Modern Weeping Prophet* (Palisades, CA: International Child Evangelism Fellowship, Inc., 1947/1953), 81.

[49]Ruth Overholtzer, *From Then Till Now* (Warrenton, MO: Child Evangelism Fellowship Press, 1990), 82.

[50]J. Irvin Overholtzer, *A Modern Weeping Prophet* (Palisades, CA: International Child Evangelism Fellowship, Inc., 1947/1953), 94.

[51]J. Irvin Overholtzer, *A Modern Weeping Prophet* (Palisades, CA: International Child Evangelism Fellowship, Inc., 1947/1953), 95.

[52]J. Irvin Overholtzer, *A Modern Weeping Prophet* (Palisades, CA: International Child Evangelism Fellowship, Inc., 1947/1953), 99.

[53]"Building a Future from the Past" in (CEF) Fellowship News, May-July, 1986, 8.

[54]One of the Dallas students was Ken Taylor, who later wrote and published *The Living Bible.*

[55]Ruth Overholtzer, *From Then Till Now* (Warrenton, MO: Child Evangelism Fellowship Press, 1990), 115.

[56]From the article "Building a Future from the Past" by Marlyn Lashbrook in *Fellowship News,"* February-March-April, 1985, p. 8.

[57]From a document entitled "A West Point for Winning Children" in the CEF archives in a folder labeled "Institute Beginnings."

[58]From a document entitled "A West Point for Winning Children" in the CEF archives in a folder labeled "Institute Beginnings."

[59]From an unpublished document entitled "Child Evangelism Fellowship Unofficial Time Line" in the CEF archives.

[60]Norman Rohrer, *The Indomitable Mr. O* (Warrenton, MO: Child Evangelism Fellowship Press, 1970), 140.

[61]"J. Irvin Overholtzer, Founder of ICEF Dies Suddenly," in *Pacific Palisades Post*, August 11, 1955, p. 3.

[62]Personal correspondence from Dr. Paul W. Rood in the archives of Child Evangelism Fellowship, in the folder marked "Mr. O's Homegoing."

[63]Paul H. Heidebrecht, *God's Man in the Marketplace: The Story of Herbert J. Taylor* (Downers Grove, IL: InterVarsity, 1990), 25.

[64]Herbert J. Taylor, *The Herbert J. Taylor Story* (Downers Grove, IL: InterVarsity, 1968), 23.

[65]Personal correspondence from Mrs. Philip Armour to J. I. Overholtzer, in the CEF archives in the folder marked "HJ Taylor."

[66]Paul H. Heidebrecht, *God's Man in the Marketplace: The Story of Herbert J. Taylor* (Downers Grove, IL: InterVarsity, 1990), 73.

[67]From an unpublished document entitled "Child Evangelism Fellowship Unofficial Time Line" in the CEF archives.

[68]Sam Doherty, *A Life Worth Living* (Lisburn, Northern Ireland: Child Evangelism Fellowship – Specialized Book Ministry, 2010), 39-40.

[69]From photocopies of a (an unpublished?) book, and from chapter 2, entitled "...He Will Do It."

[70]Ruth E. Turnwall, *Harvest Comes in Spring*, 40-42.

[71]*Forbidden Harvest*, p. 41-42

[72]"CEF Board of Trustees Appoints New Executive Director" in Newsfront: CEF News USA and Overseas, September 1971, p. 27.

[73]Ruth Marie Attaway, *The Development of Worldwide Outreach of Child Evangelism, Incorporated 1937-1975*, an unpublished paper in the CEF archives, printed in 1976, 16-17.

[74]"1977...The Year To Be Involved in Child Evangelism" in (CEF) Fellowship News, January, 1977, 1.

[75]Reese later received an honorary doctorate from Lancaster Bible College and Graduate School.

[76]New King James Version

[77]New International Version

[78]Based on a personal interview and subsequent correspondence with Gigi Graham.

[79]From a personal interview with Joni Sobels; used with permission

[80]See Isaiah 58:8-12, NIV.

[81]Based on personal interviews with Dr. Charles Schubert and with Carol Anne Hern, daughter of John and Betty McGhee; used with permission.

[82]King James Version

[83]J. Irvin Overholtzer, *A Handbook on Child Evangelism* (Grand Rapids: International Child Evangelism Fellowship, 1955), 5.

[84]Adapted from the CEF publication, *Every Child*, Volume 2, Issue 1.

[85]J. Irvin Overholtzer, *A Handbook on Child Evangelism* (Grand Rapids: International Child Evangelism Fellowship, 1955), 6-7.

[86]From a personal interview with Morris Erickson, used with permission.

[87]Correspondence from CEF of Europe Regional Director, Gerd-Walter Buskies.

[88]J. Irvin Overholtzer, *A Handbook on Child Evangelism* (Grand Rapids: International Child Evangelism Fellowship, 1955), 7.

[89]New International Version

[90]New International Version

[91]New International Version

[92]From an unpublished document entitled "Child Evangelism Fellowship Unofficial Time Line" in the CEF archives. In the original quotation the word "black" was used, but CEF uses the word "dark" to avoid misunderstanding.

[93]Adapted from the CEF brochure, "How to Use *The Wordless Book*."

[94]J. Irvine Overholtzer, *A Handbook on Child Evangelism* (Grand Rapids: International Child Evangelism Fellowship, 1955), 15.

[95]The Message

[96]New International Version

[97]The Message

[98]The Message

[99]New Living Translation

[100]There was one other time when Reese recalls getting away from the habit of tithing. He had gone into business for himself, saved up money, borrowed, and sold stock. He hadn't drawn any income from the company and was living on his savings. That money had already been tithed on, and it was diminishing. Finally he got to the point of needing to buy groceries, and he took a hundred dollars out of the company just for that purpose. Several times he withdrew small amounts as a kind of salary for necessities. He didn't think of it as income or as a wage, and he didn't tithe on these amounts. But a spirit of conviction came over him and he corrected the situation. From that point, whenever he took any money from the company he gave God His portion first. Somehow his business seemed to flourish as a result.